GW01150602

THE MOST AMAZING BOOK OF
USELESS
INFORMATION
OF THEM ALL

THE MOST AMAZING BOOK OF
USELESS
INFORMATION
OF THEM ALL

**AN OFFICIAL USELESS INFORMATION
SOCIETY PUBLICATION**

NOEL BOTHAM

JB
JOHN BLAKE

Published by John Blake Publishing Ltd,
3 Bramber Court, 2 Bramber Road,
London W14 9PB, England

www.blake.co.uk

First published in hardback in 2006

ISBN 1 84454 303 X

All rights reserved. No part of this publication may be reproduced, stored in a retrieval system, or in any form or by any means, without the prior permission in writing of the publisher, nor be otherwise circulated in any form of binding or cover other than that in which it is published and without a similar condition including this condition being imposed on the subsequent publisher.

British Library Cataloguing-in-Publication Data:

A catalogue record for this book is available from the British Library.

Design by www.envydesign.co.uk

Printed in Great Britain by Creative Print and Design, Wales

1 3 5 7 9 10 8 6 4 2

© Text copyright 2006 Noel Botham

Papers used by John Blake Publishing are natural, recyclable products made from wood grown in sustainable forests. The manufacturing processes conform to the environmental regulations of the country of origin.

Every attempt has been made to contact the relevant copyright-holders, but some were unobtainable. We would be grateful if the appropriate people could contact us.

Contents

1	Useless Words and Language	1
2	Useless Facts about Religion	17
3	Useless Facts about Numbers	37
4	Useless Firsts	43
5	Useless Facts about the Sexes	59
6	Useless Facts about Assassinated Presidents	71
7	Useless Facts about the Ancient Romans	75
8	Useless Facts about Advertising	83
9	Useless Facts about Bars and Alcohol	91
10	Useless Medical Diagnosis	123
11	Useless Facts about Royals	129
12	Useless Sayings and Omens	137

13	Useless Facts about the Universe	145
14	Sayings of Oscar Wilde, 1854–1900	185
15	Useless Facts about Geography	205
16	Useless Statistics	219
17	Useless Superlatives	229
18	Useless Facts about History	241
19	Useless Facts about Inventions	247
20	Useless Facts about Coffee	253
21	Useless Facts about Food and Drink	269
22	Useless Miscellany	297
23	Useless Facts about Hollywood	305
24	Useless Last Word	311

1
USELESS WORDS AND LANGUAGE

USELESS WORDS AND LANGUAGE

- Kemo Sabe means 'soggy shrub' in Navajo.

- The word 'honcho' comes from a Japanese word meaning 'squad leader' and first came into usage in the English language during the American occupation of Japan following World War II.

- 'Ough' can be pronounced in eight different ways. The following sentence contains them all: 'A rough-coated, dough-faced ploughman strode through the streets of Scarborough, coughing and hiccoughing thoughtfully.'

- 'Rhythms' is the longest English word without the normal vowels a, e, i, o or u.

- 'Second string', meaning 'replacement or backup', comes from the Middle Ages. An archer always carried a second string in case the one on his bow broke.

- The 'O' when used as a prefix in Irish surnames means 'descendant of'.

- The plastic things on the end of shoelaces are called aglets.

- The ridges on the sides of coins are called reeding or milling.

USELESS WORDS AND LANGUAGE

- The right side of a boat was called the starboard side because the astronavigators used to stand out on the plank (which was on the right side) to get an unobstructed view of the stars. The left side was known as the port side because that was the side where you put in on at the port.

- The term 'devil's advocate' comes from the Roman Catholic Church. When deciding if someone should be made a saint, a devil's advocate is always appointed to give an alternative view.

- The term 'dog days' has nothing to do with dogs. It dates back to Roman times when it was believed that Sirius, the Dog Star, added its heat to that of the Sun from 3 July to 11 August, creating exceptionally high temperatures. The Romans called the period *dies caniculares*, or 'days of the dog'.

- The white part of your fingernail is called the lunula.

- Oddly, no term existed for 'homosexuality' in Ancient Greece – there were only a variety of expressions referring to specific homosexual roles. Experts find this baffling as the old Greek culture regarded male/male love in the highest regard. According to several linguists, the word 'homosexual' was not coined until 1869 by the Hungarian physician Karoly Maria Benkert.

USELESS WORDS AND LANGUAGE

- The word 'set' has the highest number of separate definitions in the English language (192 definitions according to the *Oxford English Dictionary*).

- The word 'assassination' was invented by Shakespeare.

- The word 'coach' is derived from the village of Kocs, Hungary, where coaches were invented and first used.

- The word 'karate' means 'empty hand'.

- The word 'samba' means 'to rub navels together'.

- 'Long in the tooth' meaning 'old' was originally used to describe horses. As horses age, their gums recede, giving the impression that their teeth are growing. The longer the teeth look, the older the horse.

- No word in the English language rhymes with month, orange, silver or purple.

- The word 'quisling' meaning 'traitor' comes from the name of Major Vidkun Quisling, a Norwegian who collaborated with the Germans during their occupation of Norway.

- Theodore Roosevelt was the only US President to deliver an inaugural address without using the word 'I'. Abraham Lincoln, Franklin D Roosevelt and

USELESS WORDS AND LANGUAGE

Dwight D Eisenhower tied for second place, using 'I' only once in their inaugural addresses.

- The world's largest alphabet is Cambodian, with 74 letters.

- The ZIP in Zip code stands for 'Zoning Improvement Plan'.

- The side of a hammer is a cheek.

- When two words are combined to form a single word (e.g. motor + hotel = motel, breakfast + lunch = brunch), the new word is called a 'portmanteau'.

- There are roughly 6,500 spoken languages in the world today. However, about 2,000 of those languages have fewer than 1,000 speakers. The most widely spoken language in the world is Mandarin Chinese. There are 885,000,000 people in China who speak that language.

- The symbol # is called an octothorpe.

- The Paomnnehal Pweor Of The Hmuan Mnid. Aoccdrnig to a rscheearch at Cmabrigde Uinervtisy, it doesn't mttaer in waht oredr the ltteers in a wrod are, the olny iprmoatnt tihng is taht the frist and lsat ltteer be in the rghit pclae. The rset can be a taotl mses and

USELESS WORDS AND LANGUAGE

you can sitll raed it wouthit porbelm. Tihs is bcuseae the huamn mnid deos not raed ervey lteter by istlef, but the wrod as a wlohe.

- There is a word in the English language with only one vowel, which occurs six times: indivisibility.

- The seven-letter word 'therein' contains ten words without rearranging any of its letters: the, there, he, in, rein, her, here, ere, therein, herein.

- The Old English word for 'sneeze' is 'fneosan'.

- A speleologist studies caves.

- A bibliophile is a collector of rare books. A bibliopole is a seller of rare books.

- A magic potion or charm thought to arouse sexual love, especially towards a specific person, is known as a 'philter'.

- A poem written to celebrate a wedding is called an epithalamium.

- Anagrams amused the Ancient Greeks, Romans and Hebrews, and were popular during the Middle Ages.

- Twelve or more cows are known as a 'flink'.

USELESS WORDS AND LANGUAGE

- 'Aromatherapy' is a term coined by French chemist René Maurice Gattefossé in the 1920s to describe the practice of using essential oils taken from plants, flowers, roots, seeds, etc in healing.

- A group of frogs is called an army.

- A group of rhinos is called a crash.

- A group of kangaroos is called a mob.

- A group of ravens is called a murder.

- A group of officers is called a mess.

- A group of larks is called an exaltation.

- A group of owls is called a parliament.

- Cannibalism, eating human flesh, is also called anthropophagy.

- DNA stands for Deoxyribonucleicacid.

- In 1945, a computer at Harvard malfunctioned. When Grace Hopper, who was working on the computer, investigated, she found a moth in one of the circuits and removed it. Ever since, when something goes wrong with a computer, it is said to have a 'bug' in it.

USELESS WORDS AND LANGUAGE

- The study of insects is called entomology.

- The study of word origins is called etymology.

- The term 'flying on cloud 9' originates from military flights. Cloud types are classified as numbers with 'cloud 9' being a very tall thunderstorm. Jets have to climb to an extremely high altitude in order to fly over 'cloud 9'.

- The shortest complete sentence in the English language is 'Go'.

- The 'dot' over the letter 'i' is called a tittle.

- The longest one-syllable word in the English language is 'screeched'.

- There are only four words in the English language that end in 'dous': tremendous, horrendous, stupendous and hazardous.

- Men can read smaller print than women.

- The only 15-letter word that can be spelled without repeating a letter is 'uncopyrightable'.

- 'Underground' is the only word in the English language that begins and ends with the letters 'und'.

USELESS WORDS AND LANGUAGE

- The longest word in the English language, according to the *Oxford English Dictionary*, is: pneumonoultramicroscopicsilicovolcanoconiosis.

- The only other word with the same number of letters is pneumonoultramicroscopicsilicovolcanoconioses, its plural.

- The longest place name still in use is Taumatawhakatangihangakoauauotamateaturi-pukakapikimaungahoronukupokaiwenuakitnatahu, a New Zealand hill.

- Donald Duck's middle name is Fauntleroy.

- Steely Dan got their name from a sexual device depicted in William Burroughs' *The Naked Lunch*.

- A pregnant goldfish is called a twit.

- The Ramses-brand condom is named after the great pharaoh Ramses II, who fathered over 160 children.

- The letters KGB stand for Komitet Gosudarstvennoy Bezopasnosti.

- Facetious and abstemious contain all the vowels in the correct order, as does arsenious, meaning 'containing arsenic'.

USELESS WORDS AND LANGUAGE

- To 'testify' was based on men in the Roman court swearing to a statement on their testicles.

- *Can you score 3 in this quiz?*
  a) How long did the Hundred Years War last?
  b) Which country makes Panama hats?
  c) From which animal do we get catgut?
  d) In which month do Russians celebrate the October Revolution?
  e) What is a camel's hair brush made of?
  f) The Canary Islands in the Pacific are named after which animal?
  g) What was King George VI's first name?
  h) What colour is a purple finch?
  i) Where are Chinese gooseberries from?

  Now check your answers...
  a) 116 years
  b) Ecuador
  c) Sheep and horses
  d) November
  e) Squirrel fur
  f) Dogs (Canines)
  g) Albert
  h) Crimson
  i) New Zealand

- 'Strengths' is the longest word in the English language with just one vowel.

USELESS WORDS AND LANGUAGE

- Can you name three consecutive days without using the words Monday, Tuesday, Wednesday, Thursday, Friday, Saturday or Sunday?
  Yesterday, today and tomorrow.

- Quick Eye Exam…
  Count the number of 'f's in the following text:
  Finished files are the result of years of scientific study combined with the experience of years.
  How many? Three?
  Wrong, there are six. The brain cannot process the word 'of'.

- The first episode of *Joanie Loves Chachi* was the highest-rated US programme in the history of Korean television. 'Chachi' is Korean for 'penis'.

- 'Stewardesses' is the longest word that is typed with only the left hand.

- A 'blue moon' is the second full moon in a calendar month.

- Of the 17,677 words Shakespeare used in his plays, sonnets and narrative poems, he was the first to use over 1,700 of them.

- There is a two-letter word that perhaps has more meaning than any other two-letter word… and that is

USELESS WORDS AND LANGUAGE

'UP'. If you are not confused after reading this, you must really be messed 'UP'.

It's easy to understand UP, meaning towards the sky or at the top of the list but when we wake in the morning, why do we wake UP?

At a meeting, why does a topic come UP?

Why do we speak UP and why are the officers UP for election, and why is it UP to the secretary to write UP a report?

We call UP our friends, we use paint to brighten UP a room, we polish UP the silver, we warm UP the leftovers and clean UP the kitchen. We lock UP the house and some guys fix UP the old car.

People stir UP trouble, line UP for tickets, work UP an appetite and think UP excuses. To be dressed is one thing but to be dressed UP is special.

A drain must be opened UP because it is stopped UP.

We open UP a store in the morning but we close it UP at night.

When it threatens to rain, we say it is clouding UP.
When the sun comes out, we say it is clearing UP.
When it rains, it wets UP the earth. When it doesn't rain for a while, things dry UP.

We seem to be pretty mixed UP about UP.

To be knowledgeable about the proper uses of UP, look UP the word in the dictionary. In a desk-size dictionary, UP takes UP almost a quarter of the page and definitions add UP to about thirty.

If you are UP to it, you might try building UP a list

USELESS WORDS AND LANGUAGE

of the many ways UP is used. It will take UP a lot of your time, but, if you don't give UP, you may wind UP with a hundred or more.

- *Who said English was easy?!*
  The bandage was wound around the wound.
  The farm was used to produce produce.
  The dump was so full that it had to refuse more refuse.
  We must polish the Polish furniture.
  He could lead if he would get the lead out.
  The soldier decided to desert his dessert in the desert.
  Since there is no time like the present, he thought it was time to present the present.
  A bass was painted on the head of the bass drum.
  When shot at, the dove dove into the bushes.
  I did not object to the object.
  The insurance was invalid for the invalid.
  There was a row among the oarsmen about how to row.
  They were too close to the door to close it.
  The buck does strange things when the does are present.
  A seamstress and a sewer fell down into a sewer line.
  To help with planting, the farmer taught his sow to sow.
  The wind was too strong for us to wind the sail.
  After a number of injections, my jaw got number.
  Upon seeing the tear in the painting, I shed a tear.

USELESS WORDS AND LANGUAGE

I had to subject the subject to a series of tests.
How can I intimate this to my most intimate friend?

- In Finnish, *pääjääjää*, meaning 'the main stayer', has 14 dots in a row.

- And for an apt anagram finale
  DORMITORY rearranged is DIRTY ROOM
  PRESBYTERIAN rearranged is BEST IN PRAYER
  ASTRONOMER rearranged is MOON STARER
  DESPERATION rearranged is A ROPE ENDS IT
  THE EYES rearranged is THEY SEE
  GEORGE BUSH rearranged is HE BUGS GORE
  THE MORSE CODE rearranged is HERE COME DOTS
  SLOT MACHINES rearranged is CASH LOST IN 'EM
  EVANGELIST rearranged is EVIL'S AGENT
  ANIMOSITY rearranged is IS NO AMITY
  ELECTION RESULTS rearranged is LIES – LET'S RECOUNT
  SNOOZE ALARMS rearranged is ALAS! NO MORE ZS
  A DECIMAL POINT rearranged is I'M A DOT IN PLACE
  THE EARTHQUAKES rearranged is THAT QUEER SHAKE

USELESS WORDS AND LANGUAGE

ELEVEN PLUS TWO rearranged is TWELVE PLUS ONE
MOTHER-IN-LAW rearranged is WOMAN HITLER

2
USELESS FACTS ABOUT RELIGION

USELESS FACTS ABOUT RELIGION

- The Bible does not say there were three wise men, or magi; it only says there were three gifts. It is believed there were anywhere between 2 and 9 magi.

- The youngest pope was 11 years old.

- Pope Innocent X was known as Innocent the Honest because he admitted fathering his love children while he was the supreme leader of the Catholic Church, rather than just hushing it up and making them cardinals.

- Jesus was described as 'King of the Jews' as a deliberate insult to the Jewish authorities on the part of Pilate, the governor of Judea.

- 'Allah Akbar, Allah Akbar, La Allah Il Allah, La Allah Il Allah U Mohammed Rassul Allah' is heard by more people than any other sound of the human voice. This is the prayer recited by muezzins from each of the four corners of the prayer tower as Muslims all over the world face towards Mecca and kneel at sunset. It means 'God is great. There is no God but God, and Mohammed is the prophet of God'.

- The Gospel of Mary (Mary Magdalene) was discovered in 1896 by Dr Carl Reinhardt. Due to a series of unfortunate events, a translation wasn't published until 1955, when it appeared first in

USELESS FACTS ABOUT RELIGION

German. It first appeared in English along with the texts from the Nag Hammadi Library in 1977. It is missing several pages, but enough survives to draw the conclusion that at least one sect of early Christianity held Mary Magdalene in high esteem as a visionary, apostle and leader.

- King Henry I charged a tax to ecclesiastics who abandoned celibacy. The practice began in 1129.

- St Boniface is the saint that one should pray to in cases of sodomy.

- As specified by the Christian Church, the canonical hours are Matins, Lauds, Prime, Terce, Sext, None, Vespers and Compline.

- It was not until 1969 that the Roman Catholic Church quietly removed all references to Mary Magdalene as a penitent sinner and harlot, and began to refer to her instead as a disciple, although this has been little publicised.

- The tradition of Peter being the first Bishop of Rome only surfaced in the fourth century.

- Scholars estimate that the 66 books of the King James version of the Bible were written by some 50 different authors.

USELESS FACTS ABOUT RELIGION

- Almonds and pistachios are the only nuts mentioned in the Bible.

- Seven suicides are recorded in the Bible.

- Some biblical scholars believe that Aramaic (the language of the ancient Bible) did not contain an easy way to say 'many things' and used a term which has come down to us as '40'. This means that when the Bible – in many places – refers to '40 days', they meant many days.

- The Bible devotes some 500 verses on prayer, less than 500 verses on faith, but over 2,000 verses on money and possessions.

- In the ninth century, Pope Nicholas I decreed that a cockerel would be displayed from every church steeple as a weather vane. The cockerel was used to remind all parishioners of Peter's three denials of Christ before the cock crowed to keep them from this sin.

- St Augustine was the first major proponent of the 'missionary' position.

- The gospels for the New Testament were chosen from a huge selection. Many were discarded or destroyed because they did not agree with the then accepted version of Christianity. The church that came out on

USELESS FACTS ABOUT RELIGION

top simply preserved texts in its favour and destroyed or let vanish opposing documents. In some of these other gospels, we find women in very different positions — as disciples, as apostles, as teachers — than in the gospels of the New Testament.

- The Red Sea is not mentioned in the Bible.

- The Bible consists of a collection of 66 separate books. These books were chosen, after a bit of haggling, by the Catholic Council of Carthage in 397 AD — more than 350 years after the time of Jesus. This collection is broken into two major sections: the Old Testament, which consists of 39 books, and the New Testament, which consists of 27 books. (Catholic Bibles include an additional 12 books known as the Apocrypha.)

- The two robbers crucified next to Jesus were named Dismas and Gestas, though these names are not in the Bible.

- The four gospels, Matthew, Mark, Luke and John, selected for inclusion in the New Testament, are examples of books that did not carry the names of their actual authors. The present names were assigned long after these four books were written. In spite of what the gospel authors say, biblical scholars are now almost unanimously agreed that none of the gospel authors was either a disciple of Jesus or an eyewitness

USELESS FACTS ABOUT RELIGION

to his ministry. In reality, there is no evidence of these gospels' existence until the last quarter of the 2nd century, between 170 and 180 AD.

- 'Hagiology' is the branch of literature dealing with the lives and legends of saints.

- Alexander VI, known as 'the most notorious pope in all of history', often left his daughter, Lucrezia, in charge of the papacy on his frequent trips away from Rome. His papacy was marked by 'nepotism, greed and unbridled sensuality'.

- The shortest verse in the Bible consists of two words: 'Jesus wept' (John 11:35).

- The seven archangels are Michael, Gabriel, Raphael, Uriel, Chamuel, Jophiel and Zadkiel.

- Early Christians used red-coloured eggs to symbolise the Resurrection.

- In 312 AD, Emperor Constantine made Christianity the official Roman religion, and the result was the Roman Catholic Church, which is a mixture of about one-third Christianity, one-third Judaism, including the holy days and priesthood, and one-third paganism, with its superstitions, fetishes and charms such as holy water, candles and images.

USELESS FACTS ABOUT RELIGION

- Pope Innocent IV (1243–54) wasn't! He used torture to extract confessions.

- In 325 AD, Constantine called a meeting of Christian bishops at Nicaea to decide what a Christian was, and what Christians should believe. He changed the time of the Resurrection to coincide with the festival celebrating the death and resurrection of the pagan god Attis. This celebration was held annually from 22 to 25 March. Christians adapted the actual date, 25 March, as the anniversary of the passion.

- Constantine also changed the date of Jesus's birthday from spring to 25 December, feast of Dies Natalis Invicti, which was the birthday of the Roman pagan god Mithra and the biggest day of the year for the sun-worshipping pagans.

- Cardinal John Henry Newman (1801–90), one of the authorities most respected by Rome, wrote in his book *The Development of the Christian Religion*: 'Temples, incense, candles, votive offerings, holy water, holidays, and seasons of devotions, processions, blessing of fields, sacerdotal vestments, priests, monks and nuns are all of pagan origin'.

- Pope Alexander VI, a Spaniard, fathered children both before and after he bribed his way into the papacy in

USELESS FACTS ABOUT RELIGION

  1492, the same year Christopher Columbus 'discovered' America.

- Alexander VI was born Rodrigo de Borja y Borja in 1431 and was made a cardinal at the age of 25 by his uncle, Pope Callistus III, who reigned from 1455 to 1458. Once pope, Alexander VI named his own 18-year-old son a cardinal, along with the brother of a papal mistress.

- There are 49 different foods mentioned in the Bible.

- The first Patriarch of Rome to bear the title of 'Pope' was Pope Boniface III in 607 AD, the first Bishop of Rome to assume the title of 'universal Bishop' by decree of Emperor Phocas.

- At least four popes are admitted to have had illegitimate children.

- Pope John XII (955–64) is remembered as possibly the most morally corrupt pontiff. He was accused by some of turning the Rome's Lateran Palace into a brothel.

- Long ago, when many people were unable to read the Bible, pictures were put in stained glass windows to remind them of the stories.

- The patron saint of dentists is St Apollonia.

USELESS FACTS ABOUT RELIGION

- Gabriel, Michael and Lucifer are the three angels mentioned by name in the Bible.

- At least five popes were sons of priests, including at least one (maybe two) popes, who were sons of other popes! (Some of these priests may have been married but left their families to become priests.)

- At least six popes were excommunicated or condemned as heretics, including one pope who was excommunicated twice and two popes who excommunicated one another.

- In the first 12 centuries of existence, the Church was disturbed some 25 times by rival claimants of the papacy. The resulting strife was always an occasion of scandal, sometimes of violence and bloodshed.

- The longest name in the Bible is Mahershalalbaz (Isaiah 8:1).

- The Hindu holy day begins at sunrise, the Jewish holy day starts at sunset, and the Christian holy day at midnight.

- Salt is mentioned more than 30 times in the Bible.

- The letters inscribed in the Pope's mitre are 'VICARIUS FILII DEI', which is the Latin for

USELESS FACTS ABOUT RELIGION

'VICAR OF THE SON OF GOD'. In Roman numerals, the letters of this title which have assigned value add up to 666. For VICARIUS: V = 5, I = 1, C = 100, I + 1, U (or V) = 5; for FILII: I = 1, L = 50, I = 1, I = 1; for DEI: D = 500, I = 1; totalling 666 the traditional number of the Devil. (Apocalypse 13:16 says, 'Here is wisdom. He who has understanding, let him calculate the number of the beast, for it is the number of a man; and its number is six hundred and sixty-six.')

- In the tenth century, it was ruled that a cleric who experienced a wet dream would have to sing 7 prescribed penitential psalms right after the fact, and in the morning he needed to sing 30 more.

- The Assumption of Mary into heaven, which was not mentioned in the Bible, did not become Catholic dogma until being formally declared by Pope Pius XII in 1950. This states that Mary's uncorrupt body was carried straight to heaven after her death.

- Early Catholic doctrine declared that women did not have souls. Adam gave a rib to create Eve, it was claimed, but did not give a part of his soul. This belief has never been officially changed.

- In 1854 it was decided, on a majority vote of cardinals, that Mary had been immaculately conceived.

USELESS FACTS ABOUT RELIGION

The Immaculate Conception, never mentioned in the Bible, means that Mary, whose conception was brought about the normal way, was conceived without original sin or its stain. This means God protected her from the first instant of her existence so as to be free from the corrupt nature original sin brings. This is different from her being a virgin when she conceived Jesus.

- Bethlehem, which was selected by the early Christians as the scene of the birth of Jesus, was an early shrine of the pagan god Adonis. It was believed that this god suffered a cruel death, after which he descended into hell, rose again and then ascended into heaven. Each year, there was a great festival in commemoration of his resurrection.

- Many customs of the Catholic Church did not begin until sometimes centuries after the death of Christ. These are just some of them:
  The daily mass, 394 AD.
  There is no record of any exaltation of the Virgin Mary until the fifth century, when she was first called the 'Mother of God'.
  Prayers to the Virgin, Queen of Heaven, 600 AD.
  The first Pope (Boniface III), 610 AD.
  Kissing the Pope's foot began in 709 AD.
  Temporal power of the Pope declared in 750 AD.
  Worship of images, relics and cross, 788 AD.
  Holy water, blessed by a priest, 850 AD.

USELESS FACTS ABOUT RELIGION

Canonisation of dead saints (Pope John XV), 995 AD.
Lent and Good Friday began in 998 AD.
The mass first declared to be a sacrifice of Christ, 1050 AD.
Celibacy of the priesthood and nuns, 1079 AD.
The rosary introduced by Peter the Hermit, 1090 AD.
Selling indulgences began in 1190 AD.
Confession of sins to human priest, 1215 AD.
Adoration of the water (Pope Honorius), 1220 AD.
Interpretation of Bible forbidden to laity, 1229 AD.
Superstitions of the Ave Maria (Pope Sextus V), 1508 AD.
Tradition established as infallible authority, 1545 AD.
Apocryphal books added to the Bible, 1546 AD.
Immaculate Conception of the Virgin Mary, 1854 AD.
Infallibility of the Pope officially declared, 1870 AD (Decided on a majority vote of cardinals), which means the Pope cannot be in error; his pronouncements on matters of doctrine and morals are infallible and are binding upon all Roman Catholics, and they are commanded to accept the decrees of the Pope without questioning.
Mary declared to be the Mother of God, 1931 AD.

- There was a time when the Pope excommunicated members of the Church for praying to the Virgin Mary. The worship of Mary, today acclaimed as an infallible dogma, was once condemned by the same 'infallible' Church as a deadly sin.

USELESS FACTS ABOUT RELIGION

- All the teaching concerning Mary as Mother of God, Queen of Heaven, Refuge of Sinners, Gate of Heaven, Mother of Mercies, Spouse of the Holy Ghost, etc is not mentioned in the Bible.

- The first translation of the English Bible was initiated by John Wycliffe and completed by John Purvey in 1388.

- The Four Horsemen of the Apocalypse, named in the Bible's Book of Revelation, are Conquest, Slaughter, Famine and Death.

- For 40 years (in the fourteenth century), there were simultaneously up to three different infallible popes. A division occurred in the Church of Rome, and the two factions vied for superiority. One faction officially elected Pope Urban VI as the head of the Church, who was succeeded by Boniface IX in 1389 and later Pope Gregory XII. The other party elected Pope Clement VII, called historically the 'Anti-Pope', who was succeeded by Pope Benedictine XIII in 1394 as the head of the Church. Then, in 1409, a third party of reactionaries, who now claimed to represent the true Church, elected Pope Alexander V as head of the Roman hierarchy. Now there were *three* infallible popes. In June 1409, Pope Alexander V officially excommunicated the other two popes, and gradually the incident was resolved.

USELESS FACTS ABOUT RELIGION

- On 6 April 1830, in a small log cabin, 6 men including Joseph Smith and his brother Hyrum, founded and publicly signed the charter for the Church of Jesus Christ of Latter-day Saints.

- In 1844, Joseph and Hyrum Smith were led with two other men to Carthage Jail in Quincy, Illinois, on trumped-up charges. There, the jail was stormed by an angry mob of 150–200 men and Joseph and Hyrum were killed in the mêlée.

- The Mormons (led by Brigham Young) were forced to flee the confines of the United States to the Salt Lake Valley, which at the time was part of Mexico. There, they were free to live their religion as they saw fit without the constant persecution at the hands of mobocracy.

- The Church of Scientology was founded in 1953, at Washington DC, by US science-fiction writer L Ron Hubbard.

- Two bumper stickers seen in America:
'Lord, help me be the kind of person my dog thinks I am.'
'Jesus is coming! Look busy!'

USELESS FACTS ABOUT RELIGION

- 'Sensible men are all of the same religion.'
  'Pray, what is that?'
  'Sensible men never tell.'
  Shaftesbury

- To become a popular religion, it is only necessary for a superstition to enslave a philosophy.
  William Ralph Inge

- Prisons are built with stones of law, brothels with blocks of religion.
  William Blake

- I can't talk religion to a man with bodily hunger in his eyes.
  George Bernard Shaw

- It is a mistake to suppose that God is only, or even chiefly, concerned with religion.
  William Temple

- Every dictator uses religion as a prop to keep himself in power.
  Benazir Bhutto

- In matters of religion and matrimony, I never give any advice, because I will not have anybody's torments in this world or the next laid to my charge.
  Lord Chesterfield

USELESS FACTS ABOUT RELIGION

- Superstition is the religion of feeble minds.

  Edmund Burke

- Conservatives do not believe that political struggle is the most important thing in life... The simplest of them prefer fox-hunting; the wisest... religion.

  Lord Hailsham

- We have just enough religion to make us hate, but not enough to make us love one another.

  Jonathan Swift

- What a pity it is that we have no amusements in England but vice and religion.

  Sydney Smith

- Science without religion is lame, religion without science is blind.

  Albert Einstein

- Religion is the sigh of the oppressed creature, the heart of a heartless world... It is the opium of the people.

  Karl Marx

- Our religion is made so as to wipe out vices; it covers them up, nourishes them, incites them.

  Montaigne

USELESS FACTS ABOUT RELIGION

- Thanks to God, I am still an atheist.

  Louis Buñuel

- We have in England a particular bashfulness in everything that regards religion.

  Joseph Addison

- The attitude that regards entanglement with religion as something akin to entanglement with an infectious disease must be confronted broadly and directly.

  William J Bennett

- Things have come to a pretty pass when religion is allowed to invade the sphere of private life.

  William Lamb

- An atheist is a man who has no invisible means of support.

  John Buchan

- A Protestant, if he wants aid or advice on any matter, can only go to his solicitor.

  Benjamin Disraeli

- The two dangers which beset the Church of England are good music and bad preaching.

  Lord Hugh Cecil

USELESS FACTS ABOUT RELIGION

- I am always most religious on a sunshiny day.

    Lord Byron

- A lady, if undressed at church, looks silly; one cannot be devout in dishabille.

    George Farquhar

- What, after all, is a halo? It's only one more thing to keep clean.

    Christopher Fry

- Pray, good people, be civil. I am a Protestant whore.

    Nell Gwyn

- The Revised Prayer Book: a sort of attempt to suppress burglary by legalising petty larceny.

    Dean Inge

- The spirituality of man is most apparent when he is eating a hearty dinner.

    W Somerset Maugham

- Puritanism. The haunting fear that someone, somewhere, may be happy.

    HL Mencken

- There is only one religion, though there are a hundred versions of it.

    George Bernard Shaw

USELESS FACTS ABOUT RELIGION

- People may say what they like about the decay of Christianity; the religious system that produced green Chartreuse can never really die.

  Saki

- God is a man, so it must be all rot.

  Nancy Nicholson

- Baptists are only funny under water.

  Neil Simon

- There's no reason to bring religion into it. I think we ought to have as great a regard for religion as we can, so as to keep it out of as many things as possible.

  Sean O'Casey

- Every reformation must have its victims. You can't expect the fatted calf to share the enthusiasm of the angels over the prodigal's return.

  Saki

- How can what an Englishman believes be heresy? It is a contradiction in terms.

  George Bernard Shaw

- Protestant women must keep taking the pill; Roman Catholic women must keep taking *The Tablet* [largest-circulation Catholic newspaper].

  Eileen Thomas

3

USELESS FACTS ABOUT NUMBERS

USELESS FACTS ABOUT NUMBERS

- If you multiply 1089 x 9, you get 9801. It's reversed itself! This also works with 10989 or 109989 or 1099989 and so on.

- 1 is the only positive whole number that you can add to 1,000,000 and you get an answer that's bigger than if you multiply it by 1,000,000.

- 19 = 1 x 9 + 1 + 9 and 29 = 2 x 9 + 2 + 9. This also works for 39, 49, 59, 69, 79, 89 and 99.

- 153, 370, 371 and 407 are all the 'sum of the cubes of their digits'. In other words, $15^3 = 1^3 + 5^3 + 3^3$.

- If you divide any square number by 8, you get a remainder of 0, 1 or 4.

- 2 is the only number that gives the same result added to itself as it does times by itself.

- If you multiply 21978 by 4, it turns backwards.

- There are 12,988,816 different ways to cover a chessboard with 32 dominoes.

- 69 squared = 69^2 = 4761 and 69 cubed = 69^3 = 328509. These two answers use all the digits from 0 to 9 between them. As does 18^3 = 5832 and 18^4 = 104976.

USELESS FACTS ABOUT NUMBERS

- You can chop a big lump of cheese into a maximum of 93 bits with 8 straight cuts.

- In the English language, 'forty' is the only number that has all its letters in alphabetical order.

- $1 \div 37 = 0.027027027\ldots$ and $1 \div 27 = 0.037037037\ldots$

- $13^2 = 169$ and if you write both numbers backwards you get $31^2 = 961$. This also works with 12 because $12^2 = 144$ and $21^2 = 441$.

- $1/1089 = 0.00091827364554637281\ldots$ (And the numbers in the 9 times table are 9, 18, 7, 36…)

- 8 is the only cube that is 1 less than a square.

- To multiply 10,112,359,550,561,797,752,808,988,764,044,943,820,224,719 by 9 you just move the 9 at the very end up to the front. It's the only number that does this.

- The number four is the only number in the English language that is spelled with the same number of letters as the number itself.

- $1 \times 9 + 2 = 11$, $12 \times 9 + 3 = 111$, $123 \times 9 + 4 = 1111$ and so on.

USELESS FACTS ABOUT NUMBERS

- Twenty-nine is the only number that is written with as many strokes as its numerical value! (You need to write 'Y' with three strokes.)

- There are 169,518,829,100,544,000,000,000,000,000 ways to play the first 10 moves in a game of chess!

- 3,608,528,850,368,400,786,036,725 has 25 digits and divides by 25.

- 1729 is the lowest number that can be expressed as the sum of two cubes in two different ways! In other words: 1729 = 93 + 103 *or* 13 + 123.

- An 'octillion' is the lowest positive number to contain a letter 'c'.

- One is the only number in the English language to have its letters in reverse alphabetical order.

- The biggest number you can make with three digits and any operators is 9 to the power of 9 to the power of 9. As 9^9 = 387420489, the final number is 9387420489 = about 200 million digits.

- 1 ÷ 14 = 0.0714285714285714285... and 7, 14 and 28 are factors and multiples of 14 and the 5 tells you how many digits 71428 has before they repeat!

USELESS FACTS ABOUT NUMBERS

- To add all the numbers 1–10, you just divide the 10 by 2 then write the answer out twice = 55. Also all the numbers 1–100 are 100 divided by 2 written twice, i.e. 5050. This also works for 1–1000, 1–10000, 1–100000, etc!

- 144 is the 12th number in the Fibonacci series. 144 is also 12^2!

- All the numbers from 12 to 242 added together equal 70^2.

- 1274953680 uses all the digits 0–9 and you can divide it exactly by any number from 1 to 16.

- There is something curious in the properties of the number 9. Any number multiplied by 9 produces a sum of figures which, added together, continually makes 9. For example, all the first multiples of 9 – 18, 27, 36, 45, 54, 63, 72, 81 – add up to 9. Each of them multiplied by any number produces a similar result: 8 x 81 = 648; these added together make 18: 1 and 8 = 9; multiply 648 by itself, the product is 419,904 – the sum of these digits is 27: 2 + 7 = 9. The rule is invariable.

- A mile on land is 5,280ft long. A nautical mile is 6,080ft.

USELESS FACTS ABOUT NUMBERS

- A carat, the measurement of gems, is 200 milligrams, nearly the equivalent of a carab seed on which it was based.

- A pound of gold actually weighs less than a pound of feathers. Explanation: Feathers are measured in avoirdupois weight in which there are 16oz per pound. Gold is measured in Troy weight with 12oz per pound.

- If you add up the numbers 1–100 consecutively (1 + 2 + 3 + 4 + 5, etc), the total is 5050.

- What 5-digit number, when multiplied by the number 4, is the same number with the digits in reverse order? 21978; 21978 x 4 = 87912.

- The numbers 172 can be found on the back of the US five-dollar bill in the bushes at the base of the Lincoln Memorial.

- 111,111,111 x 111,111,111 = 12,345,678,987,654,321

4

USELESS FIRSTS

USELESS FIRSTS

- The first sheets of toilet paper, each measuring 2ft by 3ft, and for use by the Emperors, were introduced in China in 1391.

- The first toilet paper rolls were marketed by the Scott Paper Company in Philadelphia in 1879.

- The first child born to American colonists, on what is now Roanoke Island, North Carolina, was Virginia Dare in 1587.

- The first published American woman writer was Anne Bradstreet with *The Tenth Muse Lately Sprung Up in America* in 1650.

- The first woman newspaper editor was Ann Franklin, in 1762, of the *Newport Mercury* in Newport, Rhode Island.

- The first US First Lady was Martha Washington.

- The first magician to perform the trick of sawing a woman in half was Count de Grisley in 1799.

- The first person to cross the Antarctic Circle was James Cook in 1773.

- The first (and the only unanimously elected) US President was George Washington in 1789.

USELESS FIRSTS

- The first humans to fly and who were airborne in a hot-air balloon for 20 minutes, in Paris on 21 November 1783, were Marquis d'Arlandes and Pilatre de Rozier.

- The first parachute jump, in 1797, was made by André-Jacques Garnerin, who was dropped from about 6,500ft over a Paris park, in a 23ft-diameter parachute, made of white canvas with a basket attached.

- The first grapefruit trees in Florida, around Tampa Bay, were planted by Frenchman Count Odette Phillipe in 1823. Today, Florida produces more grapefruit than the rest of the world combined.

- The first known person to survive the jump off the Niagara Falls was Sam Patch in 1829.

- The first indicted bank robber in the USA was Edward Smith in 1831, who was sentenced to five years' hard labour on the rock pile at Sing Sing Prison.

- The first monarch to live in London's Buckingham Palace was Queen Victoria in 1837.

- The first American woman ordained a minister by a recognised denomination (Congregational) was Antoinette Brown Blackwell in 1853.

USELESS FIRSTS

- The first person to cross the Niagara Falls on a tightrope was Jean François 'Blondin' Gravelet in 1859.

- The first US President to die in office was William Harrison in 1841. At 32 days, his was also the shortest term in office.

- The first rubber band was made, and patented, in 1845.

- The first flying trapeze circus act in the world, performed at the Cirque Napoleon in Paris without safety nets, was by Jules Leotard in 1859.

- The first recognised boxing (fisticuffs) champion was Tim Hyer in 1841.

- The first US train robbery was committed on 6 October 1866 by the Reno brothers (Frank, Simeon and William), who boarded an eastbound train in Indiana wearing masks and toting guns. After clearing one safe, they tossed another out the window and jumped off the train before making an easy getaway.

- The first woman to successfully climb the Matterhorn in Switzerland was Lucy Walker in 1871.

- The first woman to run for President of the US was Victoria Woodhall in 1872.

USELESS FIRSTS

- The first woman to swim across the English Channel in each direction was Florence Chadwick in 1951.

- The first known person to swim across the English Channel was Matthew Webb in 1875. (He drowned in 1883 after unsuccessfully trying to swim across the whirlpools and rapids beneath the Niagara Falls.)

- The first world chess champion was Wilhelm Steinitz in 1886.

- The first criminal to be executed in the electric chair (in Auburn Prison, Auburn, NY) was William Kemmler in 1890.

- The first skyscraper, the 10-storey Wainwright Building, Grover, Cleveland, was designed by Louis Henry Sullivan in 1891.

- The first immigrant to pass through Ellis Island was Annie Moore in 1892. She was 15 years old and from County Cork, Ireland.

- The first woman to appear on a US postage stamp was Queen Isabella of Spain in 1893.

- The first woman to go over the Niagara Falls in a barrel was Annie Taylor in 1901. She was aged 64 years at the time.

USELESS FIRSTS

- The first bottled Coca-Cola appeared in 1899 in Chattanooga, Tennessee.

- The first woman in the British Empire to run for a national office was Vida Goldstein in 1902. She ran for the Australian Senate when women there got the right to vote in all federal elections.

- The first successful heavier-than-air machine flight was on 17 December 1903, at Kitty Hawk, NC, when Orville Wright crawled to his prone position between the wings of the biplane he and his brother Wilbur had built. The 12-horsepower engine, covered 120ft in 12 seconds. Later that day, in one of 4 flights, Wilbur stayed up 59 seconds and covered 852ft.

- The first winner of the Tour de France was Maurice Garin in 1903.

- The first land speed record in car racing was set in 1903 by Alexander Winton, at Daytona Beach. His speed was 68.18mph.

- The first Tsar of Russia was Ivan IV (the Terrible) in 1547.

- The first American woman to win the ladies singles tennis championship at Wimbledon was May Sutton Brandy in 1904.

USELESS FIRSTS

- The first winner of the Grand Prix held at Le Mans, France, was Romanian driver Ferenc Szisz in 1906, who drove a Renault.

- The first Prime Minister of Australia was Edmund Barton, in 1900.

- The first airplane fatality was Thomas Selfridge, a lieutenant in the US Army Signal Corps, who was in a group evaluating the Wright plane at Fort Myer, in 1908. He was up 75ft with Orville Wright when the propeller hit a bracing wire and was broken, throwing the plane out of control. Selfridge was killed and Wright seriously injured.

- The first licensed woman pilot was Baroness Raymonde de la Roche of France, who learned to fly in 1909, and received ticket No. 36 on 8 March 1910.

- The first reigning Queen of England was Queen Mary I in 1553.

- The first policewoman in the US was Alice Wells in 1910. She was hired by the Los Angeles Police Department and was allowed to design her own uniform.

- The first winner of the 'Miss World' beauty pageant, at the age of 17, was Alice Hyde in 1911.

USELESS FIRSTS

- The first man to reach the South Pole, beating an expedition led by Robert F Scott, was Roald Amundsen, the Norwegian explorer, in 1911.

- The first US black female pilot was Bessie Coleman in 1921. She was killed on 30 April 1926 in a flying accident.

- The first aerial combat was in August 1914 when Allied and German pilots and observers started shooting at each other with pistols and rifles – with negligible results.

- The first Miss America was Margaret Gorman, who was 16 and 30-25-32, in 1921.

- The first person to have his diabetes successfully treated was a 14-year-old Canadian boy named Leonard Thompson, who was injected with Banting and Best's new discovery, insulin, at Toronto General Hospital in 1922.

- The first to star in a talking motion picture was Al Jolson in 1927 in *The Jazz Singer*.

- The first man to fly solo across the Atlantic was Charles Lindbergh in 1927.

- The first Scrabble game was played in 1931.

USELESS FIRSTS

- The first footprints at Grauman's Chinese Theater (now Mann's Chinese Theater) were made by Norma Talmadge in 1927.

- The first Oscar winner for Best Actor was Emil Jannings in 1928.

- The first Oscar winner for Best Actress was Janet Gaynor in 1928.

- The first airline hostess was Ellen Church in 1930. She served passengers flying between San Francisco, California and Cheyenne, Wyoming on United Airlines.

- The first transatlantic solo flight by a woman was by Amelia Earhart in 1932, who travelled from Harbor Grace, Newfoundland, to Ireland in approximately 15 hours.

- The first woman to win an Olympic Gold Medal (for tennis) was Charlotte Cooper in 1900.

- The first big band, which started the swing era on radio, was Benny Goodman, on NBC's *Let's Dance* in 1934.

- The first telephone call made around the world was in 1935.

USELESS FIRSTS

- The first quintuplets to survive infancy were Marie, Cecile, Yvonne, Emilie and Annette Dionne, who were born near Callender, Ontario, to Oliva and Elzire Dionne in 1934.

- The first winner of the US Masters Golf Tournament, at Augusta National in Georgia, was Horton Smith in 1934.

- The first television service, showing three hours a day, was started by the BBC in 1936.

- The first gold record ever awarded to a recording artist was to Glenn Miller in 1941.

- The first around-the-world commercial flight was made by Pan American airlines in January 1942.

- The first canonised American saint was Mother Frances Xavier Cabrini in 1946.

- The first person to break the sound barrier by flying faster than the speed of sound was Chuck Yeager, who flew a Bell X-1 rocket at 670mph in level flight on 14 October 1947.

- The first sex-change operation was performed on George (Christine) Jorgenson in 1952.

USELESS FIRSTS

- The first monarch to have a televised coronation was Queen Elizabeth II in 1953.

- The first recorded climb of Mount Everest was by Sir Edmund Hillary in 1953.

- The first professional woman bullfighter was Patricia McCormick, who fought two bulls in Ciudad Juarez, Mexico in 1952.

- The first TV guide, in April 1953, had Desi Arnaz, Jr and Lucille Ball on the cover.

- The first woman to fly faster than the speed of sound was Jacqueline Cochrane in 1953. She piloted an F-86 Sabrejet over California at an average speed of 652.337mph.

- The first recorded person to run a mile race in under 4 minutes was Sir Roger Bannister on 6 May 1954. He broke the 4 minute barrier at Imey Road, Oxford, in a time of 3 minutes 59.4 seconds.

- The first breasts to be exposed on television were those of film star Jayne Mansfield, who exhaled at the 1957 Academy Awards and accidentally let it all hang out.

- The first living creature to orbit the Earth was Laika, the dog, in 1957 aboard the Soviet satellite Sputnik 2.

USELESS FIRSTS

- The first human in space, and to orbit the Earth, was Yuri Alekseyevich Gagarin in 1961.

- The first woman in space was Russian cosmonaut Valentina Vladimirovna Tereshkova in 1963.

- The first woman to be elected a head of state was Sirimavo Bandaraneike in 1960, who became the president of Sri Lanka.

- The first Jewish female Prime Minister and first female Prime Minister of Israel was Golda Meir in 1964.

- The first around-the-world solo flight by a woman was by Jerrie Mock in 1964.

- The first male to appear on the cover of *Playboy* magazine was Peter Sellers in 1964.

- The first human to walk in space was Alexei Arkhovich Leonov in 1965.

- The first ever nude centrefold girl was Amber Dean Smith who, in 1965, at the age of 19, was crowned 'Pet Of The Year' by *Penthouse* magazine.

- The first human heart transplant was performed in 1967 by South African heart surgeon Christiaan Barnard.

USELESS FIRSTS

- The first artist on the cover of *Rolling Stone* magazine was John Lennon on 9 November 1967.

- The first time the word 'hell' was used on television was in 1967 in *Star Trek*, when Jim Kirk said, 'Let's get the hell out of here.'

- The first woman to be placed on the FBI's Most Wanted List, for kidnapping, extortion and other crimes, was Ruth Eisemann-Schier in 1968.

- The first woman to set foot on the North Pole was Fran Phillips on 5 April 1971.

- The first athlete to win 7 Olympic gold medals was US swimmer Mark Spitz in 1972.

- The first female commercial airline pilot in the US was Emily Warner on Frontier Airlines in 1973.

- The first *People* magazine cover was of Mia Farrow in 1974.

- The first rape scene on television was in the controversial TV movie *Born Innocent*, starring Linda Blair, on the NBC network on 10 September 1974.

- The first woman to reach the summit of Mount Everest was Junko Tabei in 1975.

USELESS FIRSTS

- The first time the word 'bastard' was used on television was when Meg called her son Ben a 'bastard' in the soap opera *Love of Life* in 1974.

- The first and only US President to resign from office was Richard Milhaus Nixon in 1974.

- The first actor to portray an openly gay main character in a TV show was Billy Crystal, who played Jodie Dallas on ABC's *Soap*, which aired from 1977 to 1981.

- The first woman to qualify and race at the Indianapolis 500 was Janet Guthrie in 1977.

- The first test tube baby was Louise Brown from Lancashire in 1978.

- The first Pole to become Pope was John Paul II, Karol Wojtyla in 1978.

- The first woman chief of a major American Indian tribe, who was elected Principal Chief of the Cherokee Nation, was Wilma Mankiller in 1985.

- The first recipient of a permanent artificial heart was Barney Clark on 2 December 1982. He lived until 23 March 1983.

USELESS FIRSTS

- The first black man in space was Guion Stewart Bluford, Jr, in 1983.

- The first female Prime Minister of Britain was Margaret Thatcher in 1979.

- The first female artist inducted into the Rock & Roll Hall of Fame was Aretha Franklin in 1987.

- The first figure skater to land a quadruple jump in competition was Kurt Browning in 1988.

- The first athlete in a team sport to come out during his athletic career and admit that he was gay was British football player Justin Fashanu in 1988.

- The first woman film director to have a film take in more than $100 million at the box office was Penny Marshall, with *Big*, in 1988.

- The first lesbian kiss on television was the *LA Law* kiss between Amanda Donohoe and Michelle Green in 1991.

- The first black woman in space was Mae Carol Jemison on the *Endeavor* in 1992.

- The first woman to pilot the Concorde was Barbara Harmer on 25 March 1993.

USELESS FIRSTS

- The first female serial killer in America was Aileen Wuornos. In 1992, she was charged with killing 5 middle-aged men she met on highways while hitchhiking. She was later executed.

- The first cloned mammal was Dolly, the lamb, in 1996.

- The first person to break the sound barrier in a car, at Lake Bonneville, Utah, was Craig Breedlove, with a speed of over 760mph, in 1998.

- The first female combat pilot to bomb an enemy target was Lt Kendra Williams of the US Navy, who bombed enemy targets over Iraq during Operation Desert Fox in 1998.

- The first balloonist to fly solo around the world was Steve Fossett, who landed in Australia on 4 July 2002.

5

USELESS FACTS ABOUT THE SEXES

USELESS FACTS ABOUT THE SEXES

- A team of medical experts in Virginia contends that you're more likely to catch the common cold virus by shaking hands than by kissing.

- It is a matter of record that romantic Canadian porcupines kiss one another on the lips.

- The matrimonial pollsters contend that a man who kisses his wife goodbye when he leaves for work every morning averages a higher income than a man who doesn't. Husbands who exercise the rituals of affection tend to be more painstaking, more stable, more methodical and, thus, higher earners, it's believed.

- It has been documented that men who kiss their wives before leaving home in the morning live five years longer than those who do not.

- In medieval Italy, kisses weren't taken – or given – lightly; if a man and a woman were seen embracing in public they could be forced to marry.

- The longest kiss listed in the *Guinness Book of World Records* lasted an incredible 417 hours.

- Women can talk longer with less effort than men as the vocal cords of women are shorter than those of men and so release less air through them to carry the sound. It's a matter of breathing.

USELESS FACTS ABOUT THE SEXES

- The German language contains 30 words referring to the act of kissing. There is even a word *Nachkuss* for all the kisses that haven't yet been named.

- The average woman uses up approximately her height in lipstick every five years.

- On the island of Trobriand, a lover customarily bites off his lady friend's eyelashes. But he would never take her out to dinner unless they were married. To share a meal with her would disgrace her.

- Porn star Annie Sprinkle claims to have had sex with 3,000 men.

- Studies by Dr Karl F Robinson of Northwestern University reportedly prove that men change their minds two or three times more often than women.

- Women in nudist camps tend to use more make-up than women elsewhere.

- The first nipple rings, called 'bosom rings', appeared in Victorian Europe in the 1890s. They became fashionable among women, who often wore them joined together by a small gold chain.

- Approximately 3 million women in the USA sport tattoos.

USELESS FACTS ABOUT THE SEXES

- Until recently, among some tribes in New Guinea it was the custom for a young fighting man to give his girlfriend a finger cut from the hand of his opponent. She wore the finger on a string around her neck. Some elderly natives there still have missing fingers.

- Recent research indicates about 9,000 romantic couples each year take out marriage licences, then fail to use them.

- There are more 20-year-old virgins now than there were in the late 1950s.

- Both women and men are most likely to have their first orgasm alone.

- The US has more laws governing sexual behaviour than every country in Europe combined.

- According to a 1996 study, homophobic men demonstrate a higher arousal rate when shown gay porn than men with ambivalent attitudes towards homosexuals do.

- Among transsexuals who choose sex-change operations, females who elect to become males are reportedly happier and better adjusted after the procedures than males who elect to become female.

USELESS FACTS ABOUT THE SEXES

- Beau Brummell started the craze for ultra-tight men's trousers in the early nineteenth century. Because they were so tight, the penis needed to be held to one side so as not to create an unsightly bulge. To accomplish this, some men had their penis pierced to allow it to be held by a hook on the inside of the trousers at the time. This piercing was called a 'dressing ring' because tailors would ask if a gentleman dressed to the left or the right and tailor the trousers accordingly. To this day tailors will ask if you dress to the left or right.

- A 'buckle bunny' is a woman who goes to rodeos with the express intent of having sex with a rodeo cowboy.

- In ancient Babylon, all women were required to serve as prostitutes in the temple before getting married. Some unattractive women sometimes had to serve 3 or 4 years before finally being chosen.

- A condom will last about a month in a wallet before the rubber gets worn down by friction, making it more likely to break.

- Black women are 50% more likely than white women to have an orgasm when they have sex.

- Empress Wu Hu of the T'ang Dynasty (683–705 AD) insisted that all visiting dignitaries perform oral sex on her to pay her homage.

USELESS FACTS ABOUT THE SEXES

- In Oxford, Ohio, it's illegal for a woman to strip off her clothes in front of a man's picture.

- The most female orgasms per hour on record are a staggering 134. The most male orgasms per hour are just 16.

- Jews and atheists tend to have more sex partners than Catholics or Protestants.

- In 1869 Dr George Taylor invented the world's first vibrator, called 'the manipulator'. It was powered by steam and was intended as a cure for just about any medical problem a woman had.

- Oculolinctus is a fetish whereby people are sexually aroused by licking a partner's eyeball.

- The most successful X-rated movie of all time is *Deep Throat*. It cost less than $50,000 to make and has earned more than $100 million to date.

- In Washington State there is a law against having sex with a virgin under any circumstances (including the wedding night).

- The only acceptable sexual position in Washington, DC is the missionary position. Any other sexual position is considered illegal.

USELESS FACTS ABOUT THE SEXES

- The usual result of ingesting Spanish fly is vomiting.

- In Maryland it is illegal to sell condoms from vending machines with one exception – prophylactics may be dispensed from a vending machine only 'in places where alcoholic beverages are sold for consumption on the premises'.

- The left testicle usually hangs lower than the right for right-handed men. For lefties the opposite is true.

- In North Carolina it is illegal to have sex with a drunken fish.

- The first sperm banks opened in 1964 in Tokyo and Iowa City.

- Impotence is grounds for divorce in 24 American states.

- In Mississippi, S/M is against the law, specifically, 'The depiction or description of flagellation or torture by or upon a person who is nude or in undergarments or in a bizarre or revealing costume for the purpose of sexual gratification'.

- In the state of Utah sex with an animal – unless performed for profit – is not considered sodomy and therefore is legal.

USELESS FACTS ABOUT THE SEXES

- The average male member in all its glory is 6in long and 5in in circumference.

- In Ancient Greece young aristocratic women were deflowered by having their hymens pierced by a stone penis before marrying.

- J Edgar Hoover, Oscar Wilde, Chief Crazy Horse, Leonard Bernstein, Alexander the Great, Sigmund Freud, Lawrence of Arabia, Plato, Peter Tchaikovsky and Florence Nightingale were all gay or bisexual.

- The least expensive prostitutes in the world are the Petrapole people, who live on the border of Bangladesh. They charge as little as 10 rupees, which is the equivalent of 17 pence.

- The earliest breast implants were done in the 1940s by Japanese prostitutes hoping to entice the American GIs. They injected their breasts with liquid silicon.

- Twenty-five per cent of sexually active people engage in anal sex.

- Humans are the only species on Planet Earth to have face-to-face sex.

- In Cali, Colombia a woman may only have sex with her husband when accompanied by her mother.

USELESS FACTS ABOUT THE SEXES

- In the 1940s Dr Walter J Freeman began prescribing, in widespread fashion, a cure for homosexuality. He 'cured', to an arguable degree of success, mostly institutionalised patients. By 1955 more than 19,000 American 'deviants' had received this treatment – a lobotomy.

- Exhibitionists are most likely to be married men.

- Semen contains small amounts of more than 30 elements, including fructose, ascorbic acid, cholesterol, creatine, citric acid, lactic acid, nitrogen, vitamin B12, and various salts and enzymes.

- Women who went to college are more likely to enjoy both the giving and receiving of oral sex than high-school dropouts are.

- According to statistics, Australian women are most likely to have sex on the first date.

- The male foetus is capable of attaining an erection during the last trimester.

- The anus is approximately 4 degrees warmer than the vagina and has over 8 working muscles.

- Around the world people are having sex an average of 103 times a year. In terms of consistency, the French

USELESS FACTS ABOUT THE SEXES

get it on an average of 137 times a year. The Greeks come a close second at 133 times and the Hungarians third at 131 times per year. The USA manages an average of only 111 times a year. In Hong Kong and Singapore, they manage only 79 times, and Asia comes in last, with Japan managing just 46 times a year.

- According to CNN, a new study performed by Anthony Bogaert, a psychologist and human sexuality expert at Brock University in St Catherine's, Ontario, revealed that about 1 in 100 people are completely asexual, having no interest in sex at all.

- An excerpt from Kentucky state legislation: 'No female shall appear in a bathing suit on any highway within this state unless she be escorted by at least two officers or unless she be armed with a club'.

- When asked, white women and women with a college degree, said they were more receptive to anal sex than women of other races or without college educations.

- For every 'normal' webpage, there are 5 porn pages.

- A medical study conducted in Pennsylvania showed that people who have sex once or twice a week slightly boost their immune systems.

USELESS FACTS ABOUT THE SEXES

- Women are most likely to want to have sex when they are ovulating.

- Over 11,000 people are injured every year trying out new sexual positions.

- The smallest erect penis on record was 1 cm long.

- 'Ithyphallophobia' is a morbid fear of seeing, thinking about or having an erect penis.

- In the Aztec culture, avocados were considered so sexually powerful that virgins were restricted from contact with them.

- Marilyn Monroe, the most celebrated sex icon of the twentieth century, confessed to a friend that, despite her 3 husbands and a parade of lovers, she had never had an orgasm. So, apparently blondes don't always have more fun.

- According to a US market research firm, the most popular American bra size is currently 36C, up from 1991 when it was 34B.

- The female bedbug has no sexual opening. To get around this dilemma, the male uses his curved penis to drill a vagina into the female.

USELESS FACTS ABOUT THE SEXES

- Male bats have the highest rate of homosexuality of any mammal.

- Law in Oblong, Illinois makes it a crime to make love while fishing or hunting on your wedding day.

- Humans and dolphins are the only species to have sex for pleasure.

- Hotel owners in Hastings, Nebraska, are required by law to provide a clean white cotton nightshirt to each guest. According to the law, no couple may have sex unless they are wearing the nightshirts.

- A man's penis not only shrinks during cold weather but also from non-sexual excitement such as when his favourite football team scores a goal, etc.

- Seventy per cent of women would rather have chocolate than sex, according to a poll taken in a 1995 popular women's magazine.

- A parthenologist is someone who specialises in the study of virgins and virginity.

6

USELESS FACTS ABOUT ASSASSINATED PRESIDENTS

-USELESS FACTS ABOUT ASSASSINATED PRESIDENTS-

- Abraham Lincoln was elected to Congress in 1846.

- John F Kennedy was elected to Congress in 1946.

- Abraham Lincoln was elected President in 1860.

- John F Kennedy was elected President in 1960.

- Both were particularly concerned with civil rights.

- Both Presidents' wives lost children while living in the White House.

- Both were shot on a Friday.

- Both were shot in the head.

- Lincoln's secretary was named Kennedy.

- Kennedy's secretary was named Lincoln.

- Both were assassinated by Southerners.

- Both were succeeded by Southerners named Johnson.

- Andrew Johnson, who succeeded Lincoln, was born in 1808.

–USELESS FACTS ABOUT ASSASSINATED PRESIDENTS–

- Lyndon Johnson, who succeeded Kennedy, was born in 1908.

- John Wilkes Booth, who assassinated Lincoln, was born in 1839.

- Lee Harvey Oswald, who assassinated Kennedy, was born in 1939.

- Both assassins were known by their three names.

- Both names are composed of 15 letters.

- Lincoln was shot at the theatre named 'Ford'.

- Kennedy was shot in a car called 'Lincoln' made by Ford.

- Booth ran from the theatre and was caught in a warehouse.

- Oswald ran from a warehouse and was caught in a theatre.

- Booth and Oswald were both assassinated before their trials.

- A week before Lincoln was shot, he was in Monroe, Maryland.

–USELESS FACTS ABOUT ASSASSINATED PRESIDENTS–

- A week before Kennedy was shot, he was with Marilyn Monroe.

Useless Facts about the Ancient Romans

— USELESS FACTS ABOUT THE ANCIENT ROMANS —

- Slaves are thought to have constituted up to 40% of the Roman population.

- The slaves' standard sales contract stated that they were 'non-returnable, except for epilepsy'.

- Romans used to believe that walnuts could cure head ailments, since their shape was similar to that of a brain.

- Romans, in the third century, believed that the lemon was an antidote for all poisons.

- In Ancient Rome the law stated that prostitutes were to either dye their hair blonde or wear a blonde wig to separate themselves from the respectable brunette female citizens of Rome.

- Wealthy Romans, both men and women, would have all their body hair plucked, including pubic hair.

- Unwanted Roman babies were usually left on rubbish heaps to die.

- One Roman 'cure' for stomach ache was to wash your feet and then drink the water.

- Slaves generally came from conquered peoples, but even a free man unable to pay back his debts could be sold into slavery.

USELESS FACTS ABOUT THE ANCIENT ROMANS

- Another 'remedy' was to swallow a small amount of lead, which would cure your stomach ache, but could also kill you.

- It was an offence to obstruct the flow of water, punishable by a fine of 10,000 sesterces.

- Some Roman dishes were extremely exotic and included teats from a sow's udder, or lamb's womb stuffed with sausage meat. A recipe survives for a platter of small songbirds in asparagus sauce.

- Roman emperors ate flamingo tongues, which were considered a delicacy. They also feasted on parrotfish livers, baked dormice, pheasant brains, badgers' earlobes and wolve's nipples.

- As far as public facilities were concerned, urinal pots and public toilets served the public need. Urine from men's public urinals was sold as a commodity. Fullers (the Roman version of a not-so-dry cleaner) would empty the urinal pots and use the ammonia-rich urine for laundering and bleaching togas and tunics!

- Public toilets – rectangular-shaped rooms, some seating up to 100 people – contained rows of long, stone benches, each with a row of keyhole-shaped openings cut into it. Water running down drains underneath the benches would flush waste away

USELESS FACTS ABOUT THE ANCIENT ROMANS

into the sewers. Sponge-sticks were used instead of toilet paper!

- Asparagus was so prized a delicacy in Ancient Rome that it was rushed by chariot to the Alps, where it was deep frozen for six months to last until the Feast of Epicurius – God of Edible Delicacies.

- Ancient Romans at one time used human urine as an ingredient in their toothpaste and as a hair product.

- The Roman language, Latin, became the basis for many other languages, such as Spanish, Italian, Portuguese and French, and still influences us today.

- Rome's Circus Maximus was the biggest stadium, with seating for 250,000, and was mainly used for chariot racing.

- According to a legend, the city of Rome was founded by twins Romulus and Remus, who were raised by a female wolf.

- The Romans wrote a set of laws that became the basis for many of the legal systems of Europe and Latin America.

- They invented Roman numerals, which are still used today.

USELESS FACTS ABOUT THE ANCIENT ROMANS

- They played a wide variety of board games, including dice (*tesserae*), Roman chess (*latrunculi*), merels, *duodecim scripta*, tic-tac-toe (*terni lapilli*), Roman backgammon (*tabula*) and others.

- The Romans were the first to create sculptures that actually resembled the people they were supposed to portray.

- The Romans enjoyed a variety of ball games, including handball, *expulsim ludere*, soccer and field hockey.

- The ancient city of Rome at one time boasted 2 million residents.

- Capital punishment was often carried out in the amphitheatre as part of the morning entertainment, requiring condemned criminals to either face wild animals without the benefit of weapons and armour or, unprotected by any kind of armour, to fight each other with swords to the death.

- In the second century AD, the Romans produced glass vessels at a rate that would not be seen again in the civilised world for more than a 1,000 years.

- While 'Roman' is actually the root word for 'romance', there wasn't a lot of it in Ancient Rome when it came to marriage. There was no one to conduct the

USELESS FACTS ABOUT THE ANCIENT ROMANS

ceremony, and no legal record made of it. A marriage was recognised when a man and woman agreed to live together, or when there was evidence of a dowry having been paid.

- In ancient Rome there were two ways of telling the time: the sundial or the water clock. The day had 12 hours and the night had 12 hours. Noon was always the 6th hour of the day, and midnight the 6th hour of the night, no matter what the season, or the fact that the length of hours changed according to the time of year.

- Some Roman toilets had seats with basins underneath that emptied into the sewer system. In rare buildings, there was evidence of a cistern above the seats, so that the toilet could be flushed.

- The ancient city of Rome was on the site of the present city of Rome, the capital of Italy.

- Roman boys were educated and expected to be able to read, write and count, and, most importantly, to be effective speakers. Other important subjects taught to boys were Roman law, Roman history, Roman customs and respect for the Roman gods. Physical education and training were also important as the ancient Romans expected their young citizens to be prepared to serve and, if necessary, fight in the Roman Army.

USELESS FACTS ABOUT THE ANCIENT ROMANS

- Divorce was a lot simpler, though – you just packed up and left!

- The forum was the main focal point and meeting place of a Roman city and the site of religious and civic buildings.

- For recreation, Roman boys played at war, using wooden swords. They played board games, walked on stilts, flew kites and made models. They also played with hobby horses and hoops.

- Spartacus was an escaped Roman slave who led an army of 90,000 escaped slaves against the might of the Romans. He was eventually defeated and killed in 72 BC.

- Hadrian's Wall was begun in 122 AD on the orders of the Emperor Hadrian when he visited Britain. It was built of stone and turf, and was 80 miles long, 19 feet high and 10 feet wide.

- Most boys of wealthy Roman families would have been educated in schools away from the home, while those from poorer Roman families would have been educated at home by their fathers.

- In ancient Rome, it was considered a sign of leadership to be born with a crooked nose.

USELESS FACTS ABOUT THE ANCIENT ROMANS

- Roman boys who attended school went 7 days a week – there were no days off at the weekend. But they would get a day off when there was a religious festival or celebration and there were a lot of these.

- People would buy food on the way to and from the games, and sometimes animals that had been slaughtered in the games were quickly cooked and served to the Romans including giraffe and lion meat!

- When a Roman boy reached adulthood some time between the ages of 14 and 17, he was entitled to wear the pure white toga of a man and Roman citizen.

- Roman girls were not allowed to fall in love and choose their own husbands – a marriage would have been arranged for them by their families.

- The Ancient Romans were as fond of 'fast food' and 'snack food' as we are today. There were literally thousands of corner food shops and taverns serving food and wine in Ancient Rome.

- The Romans used to clean themselves with olive oil since they did not have any soap. They would pour the oil on their bodies and then use a strigil, a type of blade, to scrape off any dirt along with the oil.

8

USELESS FACTS ABOUT ADVERTISING

USELESS FACTS ABOUT ADVERTISING

- General Motors was puzzled when their new model Nova car failed to sell as well as expected in Central and South America, until it was pointed out that *No va*, in Spanish, means 'it doesn't go'. In its Spanish markets the company renamed the car the 'Caribe'.

- The Dairy Association's huge success with the campaign 'Got milk?' prompted them to expand advertising to Mexico. Then they discovered the Spanish translation read, 'Are you lactating?'

- Coors translated its slogan 'Turn it loose' into Spanish, where it was read as 'Suffer from diarrhoea'.

- Scandinavian vacuum manufacturer Electrolux used the following advertisement in an American campaign: 'Nothing sucks like an Electrolux'.

- Clairol introduced the 'Mist Stick', a curling iron, into Germany only to find out that *mist* is slang for manure. Not too many people had use for the 'Manure Stick'.

- American chicken-man Frank Purdue's slogan, 'It takes a tough man to make a tender chicken', got terribly mangled in a Spanish translation. A photo of Purdue with one of his birds appeared on billboards all over Mexico with the caption, 'It takes a hard man to make a chicken aroused'.

USELESS FACTS ABOUT ADVERTISING

- When Gerber started selling baby food in Africa, they used the same packaging as in the US, with a smiling baby on the label. Later, they learned that in Africa companies routinely put pictures of what's inside on the labels since many people can't read.

- When American Airlines wanted to advertise its new first-class leather seats in the Mexican market, it translated its 'Fly in leather' campaign literally, which meant 'Fly naked' (*vuela en cuero*) in Spanish.

- Colgate introduced a toothpaste in France called 'Cue', the name of a notorious porno magazine.

- An American T-shirt maker in Miami printed shirts for the Spanish market promoting the Pope's visit but, instead of 'I saw the Pope' (*el Papa*), the shirts read, 'I Saw the Potato' (*la papa*).

- Pepsi's 'Come alive with the Pepsi generation' translated into 'Pepsi brings your ancestors back from the grave' in Chinese.

- The Coca-Cola name in China was first read as *Kekoukela*, meaning 'bite the wax tadpole' or 'female horse stuffed with wax', depending on the dialect. The company then researched 40,000 characters to find a phonetic equivalent *kokou kole*, which translated as 'happiness in the mouth'.

— USELESS FACTS ABOUT ADVERTISING —

- When Parker Pen marketed a ballpoint pen in Mexico, its ads were supposed to have read, 'It won't leak in your pocket and embarrass you'. The company mistranslated the word 'embarrass' as 'embarazar' (to impregnate), so the ad read: 'It won't leak in your pocket and make you pregnant!'

- Toyota renamed their MR2 model 'MR' in France because they feared that, if the French pronounced MR2 quickly, it could sound like 'Toyota merdeux'.

- The American slogan for Salem cigarettes 'Salem – feeling free' was translated in the Japanese market as 'When smoking Salem, you feel so refreshed that your mind seems to be free and empty'.

- In Italy a campaign for Schweppes Tonic Water translated the name into Schweppes Toilet Water!

- Ford had a problem in Brazil when the Pinto car flopped. When the company found out that Pinto was Brazilian slang for 'tiny male genitals', they prized the nameplates off and substituted Corcel, which means 'horse'.

- When Vicks first introduced its cough drops to the German market, they were irritated to learn that the German pronunciation of 'v' is 'f' – which in German is the guttural equivalent of 'sexual penetration'.

— USELESS FACTS ABOUT ADVERTISING —

- For beer commercials, they add liquid detergent to the beer to make it foam more.

- Not to be outdone, Puffs tissues tried to introduce its product, only to learn that in German *puff* is a colloquial term for a whorehouse.

- Personal ads seen in America:
  Auto Repair Service. Free pick-up and delivery. Try us once, you'll never go anywhere again.
  Our experienced Mom will care for your child. Fenced yard, meals and smacks included.
  Dog for sale: eats anything and is fond of children.
  Man wanted to work in dynamite factory. Must be willing to travel.
  Three-year-old teacher needed for pre-school. Experience preferred.
  Mixing bowl set designed to please a cook with round bottom for efficient beating.
  Girl wanted to assist magician in cutting-off-head illusion. Blue Cross and salary.
  Dinner Special – Turkey $2.35; Chicken or Beef $2.25; Children $2.00

- Chrysler Corp built a compact Plymouth a few years ago, which they named the 'Volare', presumably 'to fly' in Italian, as that was a popular song at the time. Someone in the body-styling division decided, without consultation apparently, that an accent mark

— USELESS FACTS ABOUT ADVERTISING —

looked good on the 'e'. With that change, in Spanish it *could* mean 'I will fly', but it could also be translated as 'I will explode'.

- Seen on an American Airlines packet of nuts: INSTRUCTIONS – OPEN PACKET, EAT NUTS.

- Bacardi concocted a fruity drink with the name Pavian to suggest French chic… but *pavian* means baboon in German.

- On the label of Boots' children's cough medicine – DO NOT DRIVE A CAR OR OPERATE MACHINERY.

- When Otis Engineering took part in an exhibition in Moscow, a translator somehow managed to render a 'completion equipment' sign into 'equipment for orgasms'.

- 'Body by Fisher' boasted the auto giant General Motors. 'Corpse by Fisher' was how the Belgians read it.

- In Chinese the Kentucky Fried Chicken slogan 'finger-lickin' good' translated as 'eat your fingers off'.

- Label on a Marks & Spencer's bread pudding – PRODUCT WILL BE HOT AFTER HEATING.

USELESS FACTS ABOUT ADVERTISING

- On the label of the Nytol sleeping aid – WARNING: MAY CAUSE DROWSINESS.

- On a packet of Sainsbury's peanuts – WARNING: CONTAINS NUTS.

- On a Sears' hairdryer – DO NOT USE WHILE SLEEPING.

- On a packet of Sunmaid raisins – WHY NOT TRY TOSSING OVER YOUR FAVOURITE BREAKFAST CEREAL?

- On a Swann frozen dinner – SERVING SUGGESTION: DEFROST.

- Jolly Green Giant Sweetcorn translated into Arabic means 'Intimidating Green Ogre'.

- Printed on the bottom of the box of Tesco's Tiramisu dessert – DO NOT TURN UPSIDE DOWN.

- A famous drug company marketed a new remedy in the United Arab Emirates and used pictures to avoid any mistakes. The first picture was of someone ill, the next showed the person taking the medication, and the last one showed them looking well. What they forgot is that in the Arab world people read from right to left!

USELESS FACTS ABOUT ADVERTISING

- Japan's second largest tourist agency was mystified when it entered English-speaking markets and began receiving requests for unusual sex tours. When they found out why, the owners of Kinki Nippon Tourist Company changed its name.

- Microsoft Mouse was translated into Italian as 'Micro tender rat' on the instruction sheet for a Taiwanese Microsoft-compatible mouse.

- In an effort to boost orange juice sales in England, a campaign was devised to extol the drink's eye-opening, pick-me-up qualities. Hence, the slogan, 'Orange juice. It gets your pecker up'.

9
Useless Facts about Bars and Alcohol

—USELESS FACTS ABOUT BARS AND ALCOHOL—

- Alcohol is derived from the Arabic *al kohl*, meaning the essence.

- The Sumarians were the first to brew beer, and all the brewers were women.

- There is one bar in Paris that serves only bottled and canned water.

- A pub in London's West End, the Fox and Grapes, serves no spirits.

- Caesar salad has nothing to do with any of the Caesars. It was first concocted in a bar in Tijuana, Mexico, in the 1920s.

- A raisin dropped in a glass of fresh champagne will bounce up and down continually from the bottom of the glass to the top.

- To determine the percentage of alcohol in a bottle of liquor, divide the proof by two.

- In English pubs, ale is ordered by pints and quarts. So, when customers in old England got unruly, the bartender would yell at them to mind their own pints and quarts, and settle down. This is where we get the phrase 'Mind your Ps and Qs'.

—USELESS FACTS ABOUT BARS AND ALCOHOL—

- In the state of Queensland, Australia it is still constitutional law that all pubs must have a railing outside for patrons to tie up their horses.

- Many years ago in England pub-goers had a whistle baked into the rim or handle of their ceramic cups. When they needed a refill, they used the whistle to get some service, which inspired the phrase 'Wet your whistle'.

- Unlike wines, most beers should be stored upright to minimise oxidation and metal or plastic contamination from the cap. High-alcohol ales, however, which continue to ferment in their corked bottles, should be stored on their sides.

- Studying the experimentally induced intoxicated behaviour of ants in 1888, naturalist John Lubbock noticed that the insects that had too much to drink were picked up by nest mates and carried home. Conversely, drunken stranger ants were summarily tossed in a ditch.

- In Bavaria beer isn't considered an alcoholic drink but rather a staple food.

- Despite the month implied by its name, Munich's annual 16-day Oktoberfest actually begins in mid-September and ends on the first Sunday in October.

—USELESS FACTS ABOUT BARS AND ALCOHOL—

- There are 19 different versions of Guinness.

- The familiar Bass symbol, a red triangle, was registered in 1876 and is the world's oldest trademark.

- According to a journal entry from 1636, farm workers in the colony of Quebec not only received an allowance of flour, lard, oil, vinegar and codfish, but were also given 'a chopine of cider a day or a quart of beer'.

- Beck's is not only Germany's top export beer, it also accounts for 85% of all German beer exports to the United States.

- Pennsylvania has had more breweries in its history than any other state. In 1910 alone, 119 of the state's towns had at least one licensed beermaker.

- Gilroy, home of the Coast Range Brewing Company since 1995, is the self-proclaimed 'garlic capital of the world'.

- Beer and video games have a long association. Tapper, originally a 1983 arcade game and now a computer one, tests players' skills by challenging them to co-ordinate the movements of beers, a bartender, empty mugs and patrons.

—USELESS FACTS ABOUT BARS AND ALCOHOL—

- Beer-advertising matchbook covers have become sought-after collectibles on internet auction sites. A 1916 matchbook promoting Brehm's Brewery in Baltimore brought $43, while a 1930s cover promoting Eastside Beer from Los Angeles went for $36.

- An 18-year study by the National Institute on Aging found that 50-plus men who consumed a drink a day during middle age scored significantly better on cognitive tests later in life than non-drinkers did.

- In Ancient Babylon women brewers also assumed the role of temple priestesses. The goddess Siris was the patron of beer.

- Nine people were killed and 2 houses destroyed on 17 October 1814 when a brewery tank containing 3,500 barrels of beer ruptured and created a giant wave.

- According to a diary entry from a passenger on the *Mayflower*, the pilgrims made their landing at Plymouth Rock, rather than continuing to their destination in Virginia, due to a lack of beer.

- In the USA a barrel contains 31 gallons of beer.

- In 1788 ale was proclaimed 'the proper drink for Americans' at a parade in New York City.

—USELESS FACTS ABOUT BARS AND ALCOHOL—

- George Washington had his own brewery in the grounds of Mount Vernon.

- Bottle caps, or 'crowns', were invented in Baltimore in 1892 by William Painter. He proved his invention's worth when he convinced a local brewer to ship a few hundred cases of beer to South America and back and they returned without a leak.

- After consuming a bucket or two of vibrant brew they called 'aul', or ale, the Vikings would head fearlessly into battle, often without armour or even shirts. In fact, 'berserk' means 'bare shirt' in Norse, and eventually took on the meaning of their wild battles.

- The Budweiser Clydesdale horses weigh up to 2,300lb and stand nearly 6ft at the shoulder.

- Twelve ounces of a typical American pale lager actually has fewer calories than 2% milk or apple juice.

- There are 27 different styles of beer and 49 sub-styles.

- In Utah it is illegal to swallow wine served at wine tastings.

- Adding a miniature onion to a martini turns it into a Gibson.

—USELESS FACTS ABOUT BARS AND ALCOHOL—

- In 1926 Montana became the first state to repeal its enforcement of Prohibition (Prohibition lasted from 1920 to 1933).

- The longest bar in the world is 684ft (or about 208.5m) long and is located at the New Bulldog in Rock Island, Illinois.

- Christopher Columbus introduced sherry to the New World.

- The space in the New York City building that once housed the National Temperance Society is now a bar.

- Each molecule of alcohol is less than a billionth of a metre long and consists of a few atoms of oxygen, carbon and hydrogen.

- Outfitting his ship to sail around the world in 1519, Magellan spent more on sherry than on weapons.

- The founder of US campaign MADD (Mothers Against Drunk Driving) resigned after it became increasingly anti-alcohol rather than simply anti-drunk-driving.

- Vassar College was established and funded by a brewer.

—USELESS FACTS ABOUT BARS AND ALCOHOL—

- Franklin D Roosevelt was elected President of the US in 1932 on a pledge to end National Prohibition.

- The consumption of alcohol was so widespread throughout history that it has been called 'a universal language'.

- A tequini is a martini made with tequila instead of dry gin.

- Shochu, a beverage distilled from barley, was the favourite beverage of the world's longest-living man, Shigechiyo Izumi of Japan, who lived for 120 years and 237 days.

- Bourbon is the official spirit of the United States, by act of Congress.

- One glass of milk can give a person a .02 blood alcohol concentration on a breathalyser test, enough in some US states for persons under the age of 21 to lose their driver's licence or be fined.

- Fermentation within the body is essential for human life to exist.

- Fermentation is involved in the production of many foods, including bread (bread 'rises' as it ferments), sauerkraut, coffee, black tea, cheese, yogurt, buttermilk,

—USELESS FACTS ABOUT BARS AND ALCOHOL—

pickles, cottage cheese, chocolate, vanilla, ginger, ketchup, mustard, soy sauce and many more.

- The US Marines' first recruiting station was in a bar.

- The first US First Lady Martha Washington enjoyed daily toddys.

- In the 1790s 'happy hour' began at 3.00pm and cocktails continued until dinner.

- Hollywood stars Tom Arnold, Sandra Bullock, Chevy Chase, Bill Cosby, Kris Kristofferson and Bruce Willis are all former bartenders.

- Frederick the Great of Prussia tried to ban the consumption of coffee and demanded the populace drink alcohol instead.

- When informed that General Grant drank whiskey while leading his troops, President Lincoln reportedly replied, 'Find out the name of the brand so I can give it to my other generals.'

- Being intoxicated had desirable spiritual significance for the Ancient Egyptians. They often gave their children names like 'How Drunk is Cheops' or 'How Intoxicated is Hathor'.

—USELESS FACTS ABOUT BARS AND ALCOHOL—

- The bill for a celebration party for the 55 drafters of the US Constitution was for 54 bottles of Madeira, 60 bottles of claret, 8 bottles of whiskey, 22 bottles of port, 8 bottles of hard cider, 12 beers and 7 bowls of alcohol punch large enough that 'ducks could swim in them'.

- During the reign of William III, a garden fountain was once used as a giant punch bowl. The recipe included 560 gallons of brandy, 1,200lb of sugar, 25,000 lemons, 20 gallons of lime juice and 5lb of nutmeg. The bartender rowed around in a small boat filling up guests' punch cups.

- The Manhattan cocktail (whiskey and sweet vermouth) was invented by Winston Churchill's mother.

- *I Love Lucy* star Desi Arnaz's grandfather was one of the founders of the largest rum distillery in the world.

- Among the Lepcha people of Tibet, alcohol is considered the only proper payment for teachers.

- The national anthem of the USA, 'The Star-Spangled Banner', was written to the tune of a drinking song.

- In the seventeenth century, thermometers were filled with brandy instead of mercury.

—USELESS FACTS ABOUT BARS AND ALCOHOL—

- If a young Tiriki man offers beer to a woman and she spits some of it into his mouth, they are engaged to be married.

- Among the Bagonda people of Uganda, the several widows of a recently deceased king have the distinctive honour of drinking the beer in which his entrails have been cleaned.

- The Chagga people of Tanganyika believe that a liar will be poisoned if he or she consumes beer mixed with the blood of a recently sacrificed goat.

- Beer is mixed with saliva and blood for a drink that is shared when two men of the Chagga tribe in Tanzania become blood brothers.

- The shallow champagne glass originated with Marie Antoinette. It was first formed from wax moulds made of her breasts.

- As late as the mid-seventeenth century, French winemakers did not use corks. Instead, they stuffed the necks of bottles with oil-soaked rags.

- The corkscrew was invented in 1860.

- The bubbles in Guinness sink to the bottom rather than float to the top as in other beers.

—USELESS FACTS ABOUT BARS AND ALCOHOL—

- The longest recorded champagne cork flight was 177ft and 9in, 4ft from level ground at Woodbury Vineyards in New York State.

- In the nineteenth century rum was considered excellent for cleaning hair and keeping it healthy.

- Brandy was believed to strengthen hair roots.

- The purpose of the indentation at the bottom of a wine bottle is not for the wine waiter to place his fingers there, but to strengthen the structure of the bottle.

- In the USA a barrel of beer contains 31 gallons, which is equivalent to about 330 12 oz bottles or cans.

- Bubbles in champagne were seen by early winemakers as a highly undesirable defect to be prevented.

- Liquor stores in the US are called 'package stores' and sell 'package goods' because of laws requiring that alcohol containers be concealed in public by being placed in paper bags or 'packages'.

- Alcohol consumption decreases during the time of the full moon.

- Methyphobia is fear of alcohol.

—USELESS FACTS ABOUT BARS AND ALCOHOL—

- The term 'brand name' originated among American distillers, who branded their names and emblems on their kegs before shipment.

- The region of the USA that consumes the least alcohol (commonly known as the 'Bible belt') is also known by many doctors as 'Stroke Alley'.

- 'The quick brown fox jumps over the lazy dog' is commonly believed to be the only English sentence devised to include all the letters of the alphabet. Drinkers prefer, 'Pack my box with five dozen liquor jugs'.

- The word 'toast', meaning a wish of good health, started in Ancient Rome, where a piece of toasted bread was dropped into wine.

- Do you like isyammitilka or ksikonewiw? Those are the words for alcohol beverages among the Alabama and the Maliseet-Passamaquoddy tribes of American Indians.

- The first canned beer was created on 24 January 1935, and it was called Krueger Cream Ale and was sold by the Kruger Brewing Company of Richmond, Virginia.

- Drinking lowers rather than raises the body temperature.

—USELESS FACTS ABOUT BARS AND ALCOHOL—

- Rhode Island never ratified the 18th Amendment establishing Prohibition.

- In West Virginia bars can advertise alcohol-beverage prices, but not brand names.

- There is a cloud of alcohol in outer space with enough alcohol to make 4 trillion-trillion drinks. It's free for the taking… but it's 10,000 light-years away from the Earth.

- In the nineteenth century people believed that gin could cure stomach problems.

- The *Mayflower*, well known for bringing the Pilgrims to the New World, ordinarily transported alcohol beverages between Spain and England.

- Wine has about the same number of calories as an equal amount of grape juice.

- During World War II a group of alpine soldiers who were stranded in mountain snows, survived for an entire month on 1 cask of sherry.

- Johnny Appleseed probably distributed apple seeds across the American frontier so that people could make fermented apple juice ('hard' cider) rather than eat apples.

—USELESS FACTS ABOUT BARS AND ALCOHOL—

- There are 83 dry towns and villages in Alaska.

- White wine gets darker as it ages while red wine becomes lighter.

- 'White lightning' is a name for illegally distilled spirits. All spirits are clear or 'white' until aged in charred oak barrels.

- The letters VVSOP on a cognac bottle stand for Very Very Superior Old Pale.

- It is estimated that the US government takes in 14 times more in taxes on distilled spirits than producers of the products earn making them. That does not include what states and localities additionally take in taxes on the same products.

- 'Whiskey' is the international aviation word used to represent the letter 'w'.

- Most vegetable, and virtually all fruit, juices contain alcohol.

- Temperance activists, who strongly opposed the consumption of alcohol, typically consumed patent medicines that, just like whiskey, generally contained 40% alcohol!

—USELESS FACTS ABOUT BARS AND ALCOHOL—

- US President Thomas Jefferson was the nation's first wine expert.

- US President Jimmy Carter's mother said, 'I'm a Christian, but that doesn't mean I'm a long-faced square. I like a little bourbon.'

- It's impossible to create a beverage of over 18% alcohol by fermentation alone.

- In Malaysia drunk drivers are jailed and so are their spouses.

- The word 'liquor' is prohibited on storefronts in some states of the USA.

- Drinking alcohol in moderation reduces the risk of heart disease by an average of about 40%.

- US President Abraham Lincoln stated, 'It has long been recognised that the problems with alcohol relate not to the use of a bad thing, but to the abuse of a good thing.'

- The wine district of the Napa Valley has replaced Disneyland as California's number-one tourist destination, with 5.5 million visitors per year.

- A labeorphilist is a collector of beer bottles.

—USELESS FACTS ABOUT BARS AND ALCOHOL—

- British men are twice as likely to know the price of beer as their partner's bra size. A poll by *Prima* magazine found that 77% of males knew how much their beer cost, but only 38% knew the correct size of their partner's bra.

- A restaurant liquor licence in Philadelphia costs $35,000. It's a bargain compared to obtaining one in Evesham Township (New Jersey) at over $475,000 or one in Mount Laurel (New Jersey) at over $675,000.

- One brand of Chinese beer reportedly includes in its recipe 'ground-up dog parts'.

- In Bangladesh $5 will buy a beer... or a first-class train ticket for a cross-country trip.

- It takes an average number of 600 grapes to make a bottle of wine.

- Gin and tonic can help relieve cramps.

- Paul Domenech, 34, was arrested for drink-driving, but was found innocent of the charge when he proved before a jury in Tampa, Florida, that the alcohol officers had smelled on his breath was from the mixture of rubbing alcohol and gasoline that he had just used in his performance as a professional fire-eater.

—USELESS FACTS ABOUT BARS AND ALCOHOL—

- The largest cork tree in the world is in Portugal. It averages over 1 ton of raw cork per harvest, enough to cork 100,000 bottles.

- The pressure in a bottle of champagne is about 90lb per square inch. That's about three times the pressure in car tyres.

- The soil of one famous vineyard in France is considered so precious that vineyard workers are required to scrape it from their shoes before they leave for home each night.

- Gin is a mild diuretic, which helps rid the body of excessive fluid. Thus, it can reduce problems such as menstrual bloating.

- Adolf Hitler was one of the world's best-known teetotallers, while his counterpart, Sir Winston Churchill, was one of the world's best-known heavy drinkers.

- In Pennsylvania the tax on wine and spirits is called the Jamestown Flood tax because it was imposed in 1936 to raise funds to help the city recover from a devastating flood. The city was quickly rebuilt but the tax continues, costing the state taxpayers over $160 million each year.

USELESS FACTS ABOUT BARS AND ALCOHOL

- Regardless of sex, age or weight, it takes 1 hour for .015% of blood alcohol content (BAC) to leave the body. It takes 10 hours for a person with a BAC of 0.15 to become completely sober. Giving a drunk coffee will merely produce a wide-awake drunk.

- Every person produces alcohol normally in the body for 24 hours, each and every day from birth until death. Therefore, we always have alcohol in our bodies.

- The Soviet Bolsheviks (communists) imposed national prohibition following the Russian Revolution.

- The top 10 alcohol-consuming countries are:
  Portugal
  Luxembourg
  France
  Hungary
  Spain
  Czech Republic
  Denmark
  Germany
  Austria
  Switzerland

- Of Texas's 254 counties, 79 are still completely dry 7 decades after the repeal of Prohibition. Many of the remaining counties are 'moist' or partially dry.

—USELESS FACTS ABOUT BARS AND ALCOHOL—

- There is no worm in tequila. It's in mescal, a spirit beverage distilled from a different plant. And it's not actually a worm, but a butterfly caterpillar (*Hipopta Agavis*) called a gurano.

- Vikings used the skulls of their enemies as drinking vessels.

- Chicha, an alcohol beverage which has been made for thousands of years in Central and South America, begins with people chewing grain and spitting into a vat. An enzyme in saliva changes the starch in the grain to sugar, which then ferments.

- William Sokolin paid $519,750 for a bottle of 1787 vintage wine, which supposedly had been owned by US President Thomas Jefferson, then later accidentally knocked it over, breaking it and spilling the precious contents on the floor.

- Of all the countries who had armies stationed in Bosnia, only the US forbade its soldiers from consuming alcohol.

- An award-winning adaptation of *Little Red Riding Hood* was withdrawn from a recommended reading list by the school board in Culver City, California, simply because the heroine had included a bottle of wine in the basket she brought to her grandmother.

—USELESS FACTS ABOUT BARS AND ALCOHOL—

- McDonald's restaurants in some European countries serve alcohol because otherwise parents would be less willing to take their children to them.

- The entire production of kosher wine, including cultivation of the grapes, must be performed by Sabbath-observant Jews and it remains kosher only if opened and poured by an orthodox Jew.

- Thousands of waxwing birds in Sweden became intoxicated by gorging on fermenting berries. Each year about 50 lost their lives by flying into nearby windows.

- Early recipes for beer included such ingredients as poppy seeds, mushrooms, aromatics, honey, sugar, bay leaves, butter and breadcrumbs.

- Men in the USA who drink alcohol receive about 7% higher wages than do abstainers, according to data from the National Household Survey on Drug Abuse (United States Department of Health and Human Services).

- Women who drink receive about 3.5% higher wages than those who abstain.

- The USA has the strictest youth drinking laws in Western civilisation.

—USELESS FACTS ABOUT BARS AND ALCOHOL—

- In some countries the penalty for driving while intoxicated can be death.

- In Uruguay intoxication is a legal excuse for having an accident while driving.

- In Utah it's illegal to advertise drink prices, alcohol brands, to show a 'drinking scene', to promote happy hour, to advertise free food or for restaurants to furnish alcohol beverage lists unless a customer specifically requests one.

- The USA has the highest minimum drinking age in the entire world.

- Among the Abipone people of Paraguay, individuals who abstain from alcohol are thought to be 'cowardly, degenerate and stupid'.

- Kinpaku-iri sake contains flakes of real gold. While this adds a touch of extravagance, it doesn't affect the flavour at all.

- The Uape Indians of the Upper Amazon in Brazil mix the ashes of their cremated dead with casiri, the local alcohol beverage. The deceased's family, young and old, then drink the beverage with great reverence and fond memories.

—USELESS FACTS ABOUT BARS AND ALCOHOL—

- The Aztecs of Mexico used a 'rabbit scale' to describe degrees of intoxication. It ranged from very mild intoxication (a few rabbits) to heavy drunkenness (400 rabbits).

- The highest price ever paid for distilled spirits at auction was $79,552 for a 50-year-old bottle of Glenfiddich whisky in 1992.

- 'Fat Bastard Chardonnay' is a French wine label.

- The more educated people are, the more likely they are to drink.

- Research evidence from around the world generally shows that countries with higher alcohol consumption have fewer drinking problems than those where consumption is relatively low.

- Beer is believed to have been a staple before bread.

- The world's oldest known recipe is for beer.

- Early Egyptian writings urged mothers to send their children to school with plenty of bread and beer for their lunch.

- Alcohol beverages have been produced for at least 12,000 years.

—USELESS FACTS ABOUT BARS AND ALCOHOL—

- Our early ancestors probably began farming not so much to grow food, which they could usually find easily, as to ensure a steady supply of ingredients needed to make alcoholic beverages.

- In Ancient Egypt 'bread and beer' was a common greeting.

- Every year Bavarians and their guests drink 1.2 million gallons of beer during Oktoberfest. The first Oktoberfest was in 1810 and celebrated the marriage of King Ludwig I of Bavaria.

- The Romans drank a wine containing seawater, pitch, rosin and turpentine.

- A Chinese imperial edict of about 1,116 BC asserted that the use of alcohol in moderation was required by heaven.

- To the pre-Christian Anglo-Saxons, heaven was not a place to play harps, but somewhere to visit with other departed and enjoy alcoholic beverages.

- St Paul considered alcohol to be a creation of God and inherently good (1 Timothy 4:4).

- Drinking liqueurs was required at all treaty signings during the Middle Ages.

—USELESS FACTS ABOUT BARS AND ALCOHOL—

- The word 'symposium' originally referred to a gathering of men in Ancient Greece for an evening of conversation and drinking.

- Jesus drank alcohol (Matthew 15:11; Luke 7:33–35) and approved of its moderate consumption (Matthew 15:11).

- The early Church declared that alcohol was an inherently good gift of God to be used and enjoyed. While individuals might choose not to drink, to despise alcohol was heresy.

- During the Middle Ages it was mainly the monasteries that maintained the knowledge and skills necessary to produce quality alcoholic beverages.

- Distillation was developed during the Middle Ages and the resulting alcohol was called 'aqua vitae' or 'water of life'.

- The adulteration of alcoholic beverage was punishable by death in medieval Scotland.

- Rye was the first distinctly American whiskey. It is distilled from a combination of corn, barley malt and at least 51% rye.

- Mai Tai means 'out of this world' in Tahitian.

—USELESS FACTS ABOUT BARS AND ALCOHOL—

- 'Whiskey' and 'whisky' both refer to alcohol distilled from grain. Whiskey is the usual American spelling, especially for beverages distilled in the USA and Ireland. Whisky is the spelling for Canadian and Scotch distilled beverages.

- Bourbon takes its name from Bourbon County in Kentucky, where it was first produced in 1789 by a Baptist minister, although Bourbon County no longer produces bourbon.

- Gin is spirit alcohol flavoured from juniper berries. First made by the Dutch, it was called *junever*, the Dutch word for 'juniper'. The French called it *genièvre*, which the English changed to 'geneva' and then modified to gin.

- Sloe gin is not gin at all but a liqueur made with sloe berries (blackthorn bush berries).

- Vodka ('little water') is the Russian name for grain spirits without added flavour.

- 'Brandy' is from the Dutch *brandewijn*, meaning burned (or distilled) wine.

- The words 'cordial' and 'liqueur' are synonymous and refer to liquors made of sweetened spirits flavoured with fruits, flowers, roots or other organic materials.

USELESS FACTS ABOUT BARS AND ALCOHOL

- Vermouth is a white appetiser wine flavoured with a maximum of 40 to 50 different berries, herbs, roots, seeds and flowers and takes about a year to make.

- Scotch whisky's distinctive smoky flavour comes from drying malted barley over peat fires.

- Writer H L Mencken worked out that 17,864,392,788 different cocktails could be made from the ingredients in a well-stocked bar.

- Although the origins of the Martini are obscure, it actually began as a sweet drink.

- Colonial New Englanders often put barrels of cider outdoors in cold weather, then removed the ice to increase the alcoholic content of the remaining beverage.

- The Mint Julep was once a very popular everyday drink, the 'Coca-Cola of its time'.

- Most European grapevines are planted on American grape rootstock.

- Mead is a beverage made of a fermented honey and water mixture.

- Poor soil tends to produce better wines.

—USELESS FACTS ABOUT BARS AND ALCOHOL—

- 'Cocktails for Hitler' weren't drinks at all. During World War II, distillers shifted all production to industrial alcohol for the war effort. Hence, they were making 'cocktails for Hitler'.

- White wine can is usually produced from red grapes.

- No government health warning is permitted on wine imported into any country in the European Union (Austria, Finland, France, Germany, Greece, Ireland, Italy, Luxembourg, the Netherlands, Portugal, Spain, Sweden and the United Kingdom).

- One of every 5 glasses of wine consumed in the world is sake.

  In a Martini competition in Chicago, the winner was a Martini made with an anchovy-stuffed olive that was served in a glass rinsed with Cointreau liqueur.

- In Europe and North America lower-status people tend to prefer beer, whereas upper-status people tend to prefer wine and distilled spirits. In Latin American and Africa lower-class people tend to drink homebrew, middle-class people bottled beer and upper-class people distilled spirits.

- There are an estimated 49 million bubbles in a bottle of champagne.

—USELESS FACTS ABOUT BARS AND ALCOHOL—

- 'Muscatel' means 'wine with flies in it' in Italian.

- For over 25 years vodka has been the largest-selling distilled spirit in the USA and 1 of every 4 alcohol drinks consumed in the world is vodka or vodka-based.

- All 13 minerals necessary for human life can be found in alcohol beverages.

- In Welsh the word for beer is *cwrw*, pronounced 'koo-roo'.

- From 1651 until 1970 rum was issued daily to every sailor in the British Navy.

- The strongest that any alcohol beverage can be is 190% proof (or 95% alcohol). At higher proof, the beverage draws moisture from the air and self-dilutes.

- Foot-treading of grapes is still used in producing a small quantity of the best port wines.

- A *trokenbeerenauslese* is a type of German wine made from vine-dried grapes so rare that it can take a skilled picker a day to gather enough for just one bottle.

- A popular drink used during the Middle Ages to soothe those who were sick and to heal them was

—USELESS FACTS ABOUT BARS AND ALCOHOL—

called a caudle. It was an alcohol drink containing eggs, bread, sugar and spices.

- Most wines do not improve with age.

- Champagne is bottled in 8 sizes: a Bottle, Magnum (2 bottles), Jeroboam (4 bottles), Rehoboam (6 bottles), Methuselah (8 bottles), Salamanca (12 bottles), Balthazar (16 bottles) and Nebuchadnezzar (20 bottles).

- The most popular gift in Eastern Europe is a bottle of vodka.

- The Asian cordial *kumiss* is made of fermented cow's milk.

- Drinking chocolate mixed with beverage alcohol was fashionable at European social events in the seventeenth century.

- L'Esprit de Courvoisier, a cognac made from brandies distilled between 1802 and 1931, sells for around £300 a shot.

- The alcohol content of the typical bottle of beer, glass of wine and mixed drink are equivalent.

- Vintage port can take 40 years to reach maturity.

USELESS FACTS ABOUT BARS AND ALCOHOL

- British wine is different to English wine. British wine is made from imported grapes; English wine is not.

- The indentation at the bottom of some wine bottles is called a 'kick' or a 'punt'.

- Distilled spirits (whisky, brandy, rum, tequila, gin, etc) contain no carbohydrates, no fats of any kind and no cholesterol.

- Some people in Malaysia wash their babies in beer to protect them from diseases.

- Over half of the hospitals in the largest 65 Metropolitan areas in the USA have reported that they offer an alcohol-beverage service to their patients.

- A mixed drink containing carbonated beverage is absorbed into the body more quickly than straight shots are.

- The alcohol in drinks of either low alcohol content (below 15%) or high alcohol content (over 30%) tend to be absorbed into the body more slowly.

- The county in Texas with the highest DWI arrests among young drivers is 'dry' – that is, it prohibits the sale of alcohol.

—USELESS FACTS ABOUT BARS AND ALCOHOL—

- Contrary to a common misconception, alcohol does not destroy brain cells. In fact, the moderate consumption of alcohol is often associated with improved cognitive functioning. One can limit the effect of alcohol by eating and by not consuming more than 1 drink per hour. High-protein foods, such as cheese and peanuts, help slow the absorption of alcohol into the body.

- The Ancient Greeks thought that eating cabbage would cure a hangover and the Ancient Romans considered that eating fried canaries would do the same.

10

Useless Medical Diagnosis

USELESS MEDICAL DIAGNOSIS

- She has no rigors or shaking chills, but her husband states she was very hot in bed last night.

- Patient has chest pain if she lies on her left side for over a year.

- The patient was examined, X-rated and sent home.

- On the second day the knee was better, and on the third day it disappeared.

- The patient is tearful and crying constantly. She also appears to be depressed.

- The patient has been depressed since she began seeing me in 1993.

- Discharge status: Alive but without my permission.

- Healthy appearing decrepit 69-year-old male, mentally alert but forgetful.

- The patient refused autopsy.

- The patient has no previous history of suicides.

- The baby was delivered, the cord clamped and cut, and handed to the paediatrician, who breathed and cried immediately.

USELESS MEDICAL DIAGNOSIS

- The patient has left white blood cells at another hospital.

- She is numb from her toes down.

- The patient had waffles for breakfast and anorexia for lunch.

- The skin was moist and dry.

- Occasional, constant, infrequent headaches.

- The patient lives at home with his mother, father and pet turtle, who is presently enrolled in day care three times a week.

- The patient's past medical history has been remarkably insignificant with only a 40-pound weight gain in the past three days.

- The pelvic examination will be done later on the floor.

- Patient was released to outpatient department without dressing.

- The patient expired on the floor uneventfully.

- The patient was alert and unresponsive.

USELESS MEDICAL DIAGNOSIS

- Examination reveals a well-developed male lying in bed with his family in no distress.

- Rectal examination revealed a normal-size thyroid.

- She stated that she had been constipated for most of her life until she got a divorce.

- I saw your patient today, who is still under our car for physical therapy.

- Both breasts are equal and reactive to light and accommodation.

- Examination of genitalia reveals that he is circus sized.

- The lab test indicated abnormal lover function.

- The patient was to have a bowel resection. However, he took a job as a stockbroker instead.

- Skin: Somewhat pale but present.

- The patient was seen in consultation by Dr Blank, who felt we should sit on the abdomen and I agree.

- Large brown stool ambulating in the hall.

- Coming from Detroit, this man has no children.

USELESS MEDICAL DIAGNOSIS

- Patient has two teenage children, but no other abnormalities.

- By the time he was admitted, his rapid heart had stopped, and he was feeling better.

- I have suggested that he loosen his pants before standing, and then, when he stands with the help of his wife, they should fall to the floor.

- The patient will need disposition, and therefore we will get Dr Blank to dispose of him.

- She slipped on the ice and apparently her legs went in separate directions in early December.

- The patient experienced sudden onset of severe shortness of breath with a picture of acute pulmonary oedema at home while having sex, which gradually deteriorated in the emergency room.

- The patient was in his usual state of good health until his airplane ran out of gas and crashed.

- Since she can't get pregnant with her husband, I thought you would like to work her up.

- The bugs that grew out of her urine were cultured in Casualty and are not available. I WILL FIND THEM!!!

USELESS MEDICAL DIAGNOSIS

- Many years ago, the patient had frostbite of the right shoe.

- The patient left the hospital feeling much better except for her original complaints.

- When she fainted, her eyes rolled around the room.

11

Useless Facts about Royals

USELESS FACTS ABOUT ROYALS

- Saul, the first Hebrew king, was selected by the prophet Samuel to be king simply because he was very tall.

- Tsar Peter the Great made Russian peasants dig the foundations of St Petersburg with their bare hands.

- Mary Stuart became Queen of Scotland when she was only 6 days old.

- Every queen named Jane has either been murdered, imprisoned, gone mad, died young or been dethroned.

- Queen Elizabeth II was an 18-year-old mechanic in the English military during World War II.

- King Edward VII was so enthusiastic about his shooting that he arranged for all of the 180 or so clocks on the Sandringham Estate to be set half-an-hour early to allow him more time for his sport. Anyone having business with the King needed to ensure they kept their appointment to 'Sandringham Time'. George V maintained this same tradition throughout his reign. However, when Edward VIII took the throne in 1936, he arranged for all of the clocks to be reset and kept in line with those in the rest of his kingdom.

USELESS FACTS ABOUT ROYALS

- Queen Elizabeth I regarded herself as a paragon of cleanliness. She declared that she bathed once every 3 months, whether she needed it or not.

- Each king in a deck of playing cards represents a great king from history. Spades – King David, Clubs – Alexander the Great, Hearts – Charlemagne, and Diamonds – Julius Caesar.

- The movie *The Madness of King George III* was released in America under the title *The Madness of King George*, because it was believed that American moviegoers would believe it to be a sequel and would not go to see it because they had never seen *The Madness of King George I and II*.

- King George I of England could not speak English. He was born and raised in Germany, and never learned to speak English even though he was king from 1714 to 1727. The King left the running of the country to his ministers, thereby creating the first government cabinet.

- Queen Anne had a transvestite cousin, Lord Cornbury, whom she assigned to be governor of New York and New Jersey. The colonists were not amused.

- Anne Boleyn, Queen Elizabeth I's mother, had 6 fingers on one hand.

USELESS FACTS ABOUT ROYALS

- In the fourteenth century, King Edward II was deposed in favour of his son, Edward III, and later killed. In order not to mark his body, and hide evidence of murder, a deer horn was inserted into his rectum and a red-hot poker placed inside that. His ghostly screams are said still to be heard in the castle.

- Queen Anne (1665–1714) outlived all 17 of her children.

- Sir Walter Raleigh financed his trip to America to cultivate tobacco by betting Queen Elizabeth I that he could weigh the weight of smoke. He did so by placing 2 identical cigars on opposite sides of a scale, lighting 1 and making sure no ashes fell. The difference in the weight after the cigar was finished was the weight of smoke and Raleigh was on his way to America.

- Prince Harry and Prince William are uncircumcised.

- King Alfonso of Spain (1886–1931) was so tone-deaf that he had one man in his employ known as the 'Anthem Man', whose duty it was to tell the King to stand up whenever the Spanish national anthem was played because the Monarch couldn't recognise it.

- The Spanish kingdom of Castile once had a reigning queen who had been a nun. She was Doña Urraca of

USELESS FACTS ABOUT ROYALS

the house of Navarre, daughter of Alfonso the VI of Leon and Castile, and reigned from 1109 to 1126. Eventually she married and had a son, who took the throne when she died.

- King Louis the XIV, also known as the Sun King, was almost certainly not the son of Louis the XIII, but the son of the Danish nobleman Josiah Rantzau, who served in France as a general and marechal of France. He had to leave France when the boy grew up because Louis was his spitting image.

- Pepin the Short, King of the Franks (751–768 AD) was 4ft 6in tall. His wife was known as Bertha of the Big Foot.

- In her entire lifetime Queen Isabella of Spain (1451–1504) bathed twice.

- When Elizabeth I of Russia died in 1762, 15,000 dresses were found in her closets. She used to change what she was wearing two or even three times an evening.

- Czar Paul I of Russia banished soldiers to Siberia for marching out of step.

- Catherine the Great of Russia, known as 'The Enlightened Despot', relaxed by being tickled.

USELESS FACTS ABOUT ROYALS

- King Louis XV was the first person to use a lift; in 1743 his 'flying chair' carried him between the floors of the Versailles Palace.

- The reign of Czar Nicholas II of Russia ended in tragedy in 1918, when he and his family were murdered, but it had started badly as well. At his coronation, presents were given to all those who attended. But a rumour started that there weren't enough to go around and, in the stampede that followed, hundreds of women and children were killed.

- Queen Supayalat of Burma ordered about 100 of her husband's relatives to be clubbed to death to ensure he had no contenders for the throne.

- While performing her duties as queen, Cleopatra sometimes wore a fake beard.

- After Sir Walter Raleigh introduced tobacco into England in the early seventeenth century, King James I wrote a booklet against smoking.

- Queen Elizabeth II was *Time* magazine's 'Man of The Year' in 1952.

- King Charles VII, who was assassinated in 1167, was the first Swedish king with the name of Charles. Charles I, II, III, IV, V and VI never existed. No one

USELESS FACTS ABOUT ROYALS

knows why. To add to the mystery, almost 300 years went by before there was a Charles VIII (1448–57).

- If the arm of King Henry I had been 42in long, the unit of measure of a 'foot' today would be 14in. But his arm happened to be 36in long and he decreed that the 'standard' foot should be one-third that length: 12in.

- Queen Lydia Liliuokalani was the last reigning monarch of the Hawaiian Islands. She was also the only Queen the United States ever had.

- Queen Victoria used marijuana to help relieve menstrual cramp pain.

- When Queen Elizabeth I died, she owned over 3,000 gowns.

- Prince Philip, the Duke of Edinburgh, names his dogs after orchestral conductors.

12

USELESS SAYINGS AND OMENS

USELESS SAYINGS AND OMENS

- You will have bad luck if you don't get out of bed on the same side that you got in.

- Wear a blue bead to protect yourself from witches.

- It is bad luck to place a hat on the bed.

- A necklace of amber beads protects against illness and colds.

- A bird entering the house is a sign of death.

- It is bad luck to take a broom with you when you move. Always throw out the old and buy a new one.

- If you see three butterflies together, it will bring you luck.

- Make a wish if you meet a chimney sweep by chance and it will come true.

- When cows lift their tails, it is a sign that rain is on the way.

- If you bid farewell to a friend while standing on a bridge, you will never see each other again.

- It is bad luck to turn a loaf of bread upside down once a slice has been removed.

USELESS SAYINGS AND OMENS

- Leaving a house by a different door to the one you used on entry brings bad luck.

- If you dream of fish, then someone you know is pregnant.

- You can avoid headaches for the year to come by having your hair cut on Good Friday.

- Letting milk boil over brings bad luck.

- An itch in your right palm means you will soon be receiving money. However, an itch in the left palm means you will be soon paying money out.

- Saying the word 'pig' while fishing at sea brings bad luck.

- A major row with your best friend will follow if you spill pepper.

- If you catch a falling leaf in autumn you won't get a cold all winter.

- Planting rosemary by the front door keeps witches away.

- If you drop a pair of scissors, then your lover is being unfaithful.

USELESS SAYINGS AND OMENS

- Seeing an owl in sunlight is bad luck.

- Crossed knives on a table mean a quarrel.

- A wish made when you see a shooting star will come true.

- If you knit some of your own hairs into a garment, then the recipient will be bound to you.

- Mirrors should be covered during a thunderstorm as they attract lightning.

- When three people are photographed together, the one in the middle will die first.

- When you sneeze, place a hand in front of your mouth to prevent your soul escaping.

- It is bad luck to open an umbrella indoors, especially if you put it over your head.

- If a dead person's eyes are left open, he will find someone to take with him.

- It is bad luck to count the cars in a funeral cortege.

- If you bite your tongue while eating, it shows you have recently told a lie.

USELESS SAYINGS AND OMENS

- It is bad luck to wear opals unless you were born in October.

- All windows should be opened the moment someone dies so their soul can leave.

- If you dream of death it's a sign of birth, and if you dream of birth it's a sign of death.

- It is very bad luck to wear something new to a funeral, especially new shoes.

- To bring luck, the first gift a bride opens should be the first gift she uses.

- The person who gives the third wedding gift to be opened by a bride will soon have a baby.

- If the groom drops the wedding ring during the wedding ceremony, the marriage is doomed.

- Seeing a black cat or a chimney sweep on the way to a wedding is very lucky.

- If a girl sleeps with a piece of a friend's wedding cake under her pillow she will dream of her future husband.

- It is bad luck to let a flag touch the ground.

USELESS SAYINGS AND OMENS

- An acorn carried in your pocket brings good luck and long life.

- Spitting on a new cricket bat before using it makes it lucky.

- If a swarm of bees nests in the roof, it means the house will burn down.

- If you sweep out the room occupied by an unwelcome guest, then it will prevent their returning.

- A black cat walking towards you brings good luck. Walking away from you it takes the luck with it.

- It is bad luck to step on a crack in the pavement.

- Pulling out a grey or white hair will cause 10 to grow in its place.

- Ivy on the walls of a house protects the occupants from witches and evil spirits.

- Dropping an umbrella on the floor means there will be a murder in the house.

- It is bad luck to spill salt, unless you throw a pinch of it over your left shoulder, into the face of the Devil waiting there.

USELESS SAYINGS AND OMENS

- It is bad luck to kill a ladybird.

- You must hold your breath when walking past a cemetery or you will breathe in the spirit of someone who recently died.

- Thunder immediately following a funeral means the dead person's soul has reached heaven.

- An acorn on the windowsill will prevent lightning striking.

- It is unlucky to see your face in a mirror by candlelight.

- To know the number of children you will have, cut an apple in half and count the number of pips.

- When a bell rings, a new angel has received his wings.

- If the first butterfly you see in a year is white, then you will have good luck all year.

- If your right ear itches, someone is speaking well of you. If your left ear itches, they are speaking badly of you.

- A knife placed under the bed during childbirth will ease the pain of labour.

USELESS SAYINGS AND OMENS

- A raw onion cut in half and placed under a sick person's bed will draw off fever and poisons.

- Use the same pencil for a test as you use to study for it, and it will remember the answers.

- Putting salt on the doorstep of a new house stops evil from entering.

- A woman buried in black will return to haunt the family.

- Mirrors in a house with a corpse should be covered or the person who sees himself will die next.

- Seeing an ambulance is very unlucky unless you hold your breath or pinch your nose until you see a black or brown dog.

- Starting a trip on a Friday means you will meet misfortune.

13

USELESS FACTS ABOUT THE UNIVERSE

—USELESS FACTS ABOUT THE UNIVERSE—

- Venus spins the opposite way to the other planets.

- The brightest star in the night sky is Sirius. Also known as the Dog Star, it is 51 trillion miles from the Earth or about 8.7 light-years. The second brightest star is Canopus, which is only visible in the Southern Hemisphere.

- To reach outer space, you need to travel at least 50 miles from the Earth's surface.

- Mars was named after the Roman god of war.

- The largest asteroid on record is Ceres. It is so big it would stretch a distance of over 600 miles!

- Jupiter has no solid surface, only layers of gaseous clouds. It is composed mainly of hydrogen and helium.

- The average size of a meteor is no bigger than a grain of sand.

- The Earth spins faster on its axis in September than it does in March.

- The far side of the Moon was first photographed by a Russian satellite in 1959.

- The diameter of the Moon is 3,476km.

USELESS FACTS ABOUT THE UNIVERSE

- Mariner 10 was the first spacecraft to fly by Mercury. In 1974 it sent back close-up pictures of a world that resembles our Moon.

- The surface temperature of Venus is hot enough to melt lead! Lead melts at 662°F and the surface can reach temperatures of 864°F (462°C).

- Ninety-nine per cent of our solar system's mass is concentrated in the Sun.

- The Moon has about 3 trillion craters larger than 3ft in diameter.

- It takes Jupiter almost 12 Earth years to orbit the Sun. The length of a day on Jupiter is 9 hours 50 minutes 30 seconds at the equator.

- Uranus is visible to the naked eye.

- The Moon orbits the Earth every 27.32 days.

- It takes 8.5 minutes for light to get from the Sun to the Earth.

- The Earth is the only planet not named after a god.

- On a clear night, over 2,000 stars are visible to the naked eye.

—USELESS FACTS ABOUT THE UNIVERSE—

- The Sun's mass decreases by 4,000,000 tons per second due to conversion of hydrogen to helium by thermonuclear reaction; this conversion will continue for another 5,000 million years before the Sun's energy supply is exhausted.

- Due to gravitational effects, you weigh slightly less when the Moon is directly overhead.

- Uranus was only discovered 225 years ago, on 13 March 1781, by Sir William Herschel.

- The Milky Way galaxy contains 5 billion stars larger than our Sun.

- Our galaxy is 75,000 light-years in diameter and our Sun is 26,100 light-years from the centre.

- Based on various cosmological techniques, the universe is estimated at 10–18 gigayears old (1 gigayear = 1,000,000,000,000 years).

- The smallest star found to date is a neutron star, with a diameter of 59km but a mass of 10 times that of our Sun. This star is more commonly known as a black hole.

- The Earth's average velocity orbiting the Sun is 107,220km per hour.

USELESS FACTS ABOUT THE UNIVERSE

- Driving at 75mph (121km), it would take 258 days to drive around one of Saturn's rings.

- The Sun has a core temperature of 154,000,000 Kelvin.

- Because of a large orbital eccentricity, Pluto was closer to the Sun than Neptune between January 1979 and March 1999.

- Mars has a volcano (Olympus Mons), which is 310–70 miles in diameter and 16 miles high.

- The Earth is the densest planet in the solar system.

- The Future's Museum in Sweden contains a scale model of the solar system. The Sun is 105m in diameter and the planets range from 3.5mm to 6km from the Sun. This particular model also contains the nearest star, Proxima Centauri, still to scale situated in the Museum of Victoria in Australia.

- The maximum possible duration of an eclipse is 7 minutes and 31 seconds.

- So far in the twentieth century, two objects have hit the Earth's surface with enough force to destroy a medium-size city. By pure luck, both have landed in sparsely populated Siberia.

— USELESS FACTS ABOUT THE UNIVERSE —

- Copernicus's book, which suggested that the Sun and not the Earth was the centre of the solar system, was officially banned by the papacy until 1835.

- Our own galaxy is minute compared to the radio galaxies being discovered at the edge of the universe.

- Scientists believe that hydrogen comprises approximately 90–99% of all matter in the universe.

- The Sun is 330,330 times larger than the Earth.

- Without using precision instruments, Eratosthenes measured the radius of the Earth in the third century BC, and came within 1% of the value determined by today's technology.

- Venus does not tilt as it goes around the Sun, so it has no seasons. On Mars, however, the seasons are more exaggerated and last much longer than on Earth.

- Venus is named after the Roman goddess of love.

- Scientists have determined that most rocks on the surface of the Moon are between 3 and 4.6 billion years old.

- The point in a lunar orbit that is farthest from the moon is called an apolune.

—USELESS FACTS ABOUT THE UNIVERSE—

- Selenologists are those who study the Moon.

- The pressure at the centre of the Earth is 27,000 tons per square inch. At the centre of the giant planet Jupiter, the pressure is three times as great.

- The Sea of Tranquillity on the Moon is not a real sea, but a 'maria', one of the regions on the Moon that appear dark when you look at it.

- The star Alpha Herculis is 25 times larger than the circumference described by the Earth's revolution around the Sun.

- Uranus, the 7th planet from the Sun, is tipped on its side so that at any moment one pole is pointed at the Sun. The polar regions are warmer than the equator. At the poles, a day lasts for 42 Earth years, followed by an equally long night.

- The size of the first footprint on the Moon was 13 x 6 in, the dimensions of Neil Armstrong's boot when he took his historic walk on 20 July 1969.

- Pluto, the smallest planet in our solar system, is a little smaller than the Earth's Moon.

- The solar wind flows past the Earth at 1,200 times the speed of sound.

—USELESS FACTS ABOUT THE UNIVERSE—

- The smallest visible sunspots have an area of 500 million square miles, about 50 times the size of Africa. The largest sunspots have an area of about 7,000 million square miles.

- The Sun gives off a stream of electrically charged particles called the solar wind. Every second, the Sun pumps more than a million tons of material into the solar wind.

- 'Ufology' is the study of UFOs, especially those thought to be from outer space.

- A brown dwarf is a very small dark object, with a mass less than one-tenth that of the Sun. They are 'failed stars' – globules of gas that have shrunk under gravity, but failed to ignite and shine as stars.

- A cosmic year is the amount of time it takes the Sun to revolve around the centre of the Milky Way, about 225 million years.

- The star Antares is 60,000 times larger than our Sun. If our Sun were the size of a softball, the star Antares would be as large as a house.

- A bucket filled with earth would weigh about five times more than the same bucket filled with the substance of the Sun. However, the force of gravity is

USELESS FACTS ABOUT THE UNIVERSE

so much greater on the Sun that a man weighing 150lb on Earth would weigh 2 tons on the Sun.

- A car travelling at a constant speed of 60mph would take longer than 48 million years to reach the nearest star (other than our Sun), Proxima Centauri. This is about 685,000 average human lifetimes.

- The star known as LP 327-186, a so-called white dwarf, is smaller than the state of Texas, yet so dense that, if a cubic inch of it were brought to Earth, it would weigh more than 1.5 million tons.

- The star Sirius B is so dense a handful of it weighs about one million pounds.

- There are 100,000 million stars in our galaxy.

- The Sun contains over 99.8% of the total mass in our solar system, while Jupiter contains most of the rest. The fractional percentage that is left is made up of our Earth and Moon and the remaining planets and asteroids.

- The discovery of Neptune was announced in 1846. But, when astronomers checked previous records, they found the record of an observation of the planet as far back as 1795 by astronomers who, believing it to be a star, recorded the position routinely.

—USELESS FACTS ABOUT THE UNIVERSE—

- Since Neptune's discovery in 1846, it has made about three-quarters of one revolution of the Sun.

- The pressure at the centre of the Sun is about 700 million tons per square inch. It's enough to smash atoms, expose the inner nuclei and allow them to smash into each other, interact and produce the radiation that gives off light and warmth.

- The reflecting power of a planet or satellite, expressed as a ratio of reflected light to the total amount falling on the surface, is called the albedo.

- The star Zeta Thaun, a supernova, was so bright when it exploded in 1054 that it could be seen during the day.

- The Sun is 93 million miles from Earth, yet it is 270,000 times closer than the next nearest star.

- A day on Mercury is twice as long as its year. Mercury rotates very slowly but revolves around the Sun in slightly less than 88 days.

- A galaxy of typical size – about 100 billion suns – produces less energy than a single quasar.

- A solar day on Mercury, from sunrise to sunset, lasts about 6 Earth months.

USELESS FACTS ABOUT THE UNIVERSE

- The Sun is about midway in the scale of star sizes, but most are smaller ones. Only 5% of the stars in our galaxy are larger than the Sun. (That's still 5 billion larger stars.)

- A neutron star is the strongest magnet in the universe. The magnetic field of a neutron star is a million million times stronger than the Earth's magnetism.

- About 20 new stars are born in our galaxy each year.

- A pulsar is a small star made up of neutrons so densely packed together that, if one the size of a ten-pence piece landed on Earth, it would weigh approximately 100 million tons.

- A space shuttle at lift-off develops more power than all the cars in England combined.

- A spectroheliokinematograph is a special camera used to film the Sun.

- Afternoon temperatures on Mars go up to about 80°F in some areas, and down to -190° F at night.

- A sunbeam setting out through space at the rate of 186,000 miles a second would describe a gigantic circle and return to its origins after about 200 billion years.

USELESS FACTS ABOUT THE UNIVERSE

- A typical nova explosion releases about as much energy as the Sun emits in 10,000 years, or as much as in 1,000,000,000,000,000,000,000 nuclear bombs.

- A white dwarf has a mass equal to that of the Sun, but a diameter only about that of the Earth. A cupful of white dwarf material weighs about 22 tons, the same as 5 elephants.

- About 40 novae erupt in our galaxy each year.

- Two of every three stars in the galaxy are binary, meaning pairs of stars are more common than single-star systems like our own.

- Gold exists on Mars, Mercury and Venus.

- All the coal, oil, gas and wood on Earth would only keep the Sun burning for a few days.

- All the planets in our solar system could be placed inside the planet Jupiter. Jupiter is two and a half times larger than all the other planets, satellites, asteroids and comets of our solar system combined.

- If one were to capture and bottle a comet's 10,000-mile vapour trail, the amount of vapour actually present in the bottle would take up less than 1 cubic inch of space.

—USELESS FACTS ABOUT THE UNIVERSE—

- Although the Sun is 400 times larger than the Moon, it appears the same size in the sky because it is 400 times further away.

- An area of the Sun's surface the size of a postage stamp shines with the power of 1,500,000 candles.

- An estimated 10,000 million of the 100,000 million stars in our galaxy have died and produced white dwarfs.

- An object weighing 100lb on Earth would weigh just 38lb on Mars.

- If the Earth was the size of an apple, the atmospheric layer would be no thicker than the skin of the apple.

- If our whole galaxy were the size of a 10-pence piece, our solar system would be smaller than the size of a molecule. Other galaxies would be from 1ft to 1,000ft away.

- If the world were to become totally flat and the oceans distributed themselves evenly over the Earth's surface, the water would be approximately 2 miles deep at every point.

- Asteroids smaller than 600ft across entering the Earth's atmosphere burn away and lose most of their energy

—USELESS FACTS ABOUT THE UNIVERSE—

before hitting our planet. But even these smaller objects can cause devastation. A small asteroid exploded in the air in Siberia in 1908. The resulting shock wave flattened 800 square miles of forest. The detonation's force was estimated to have been 1,000 times greater than the Hiroshima bomb.

- Ancient Chinese astronomers first observed sunspots about 2,000 years ago. Westerners took quite a while to catch up, first writing of the dark blotches 1,700 years later, and wrongly believing them to be small planets.

- Antarctica has been used as a testing laboratory for the joint United States–Soviet Union mission to Mars because it has much in common with the red planet.

- Aristarchus, a Greek astronomer living about 200 BC, was reportedly the first person to declare that the Earth revolved around the Sun. His theory was disregarded for hundreds of years.

- Arthur C Clarke, in 1959, made a bet that the first man to land on the Moon would do so by June 1969. US astronauts landed on 20 July 1969.

- At its centre, the Sun has a density of over 100 times that of water, and a temperature of 10–20 million degrees Celsius.

— USELESS FACTS ABOUT THE UNIVERSE —

- If you attempted to count the stars in a galaxy at a rate of one every second, it would take around 3,000 years to count them all.

- If you drove a car from Earth at a constant speed of 100mph, it would take about 221,000 million years to reach the centre of the Milky Way.

- If you travelled to Proxima Centauri, the star nearest to the Earth (outside our solar system), the Sun would appear to be a bright star in the constellation of Cassiopeia.

- In 1066 Halley's Comet appeared shortly before William the Conqueror invaded England. The Norman king took it as a good omen; his battle cry became 'A new star, a new king'.

- In 1937 the tiny asteroid Hermes passed uncomfortably close to the Earth, at a distance of less than twice that of the Moon.

- Astronomers believe Jupiter's moon, Europa, may have an ocean of liquid water beneath an ice cap.

- At the end of every 19 years, the lunar phases repeat themselves. In effect, the tide tables for the next 19 years will be approximately the same as those for the past 19 years.

—USELESS FACTS ABOUT THE UNIVERSE—

- At midday on Mercury, the sunlight is hot enough to melt lead.

- Small satellites within a planet's rings are sometimes called 'mooms'.

- Some astronomers believe Pluto's strange and erratic orbit indicates that it wasn't one of the original planets at all, but rather a moon of Neptune that somehow broke loose.

- In 1994 the comet Shoemaker-Levy 9 broke apart and plunged into Jupiter, ripping holes the size of Earth in the planet's atmosphere.

- Some neutron stars spin 600 times a second, which is as fast as a dentist's drill.

- Space dust is extremely small – smaller than a particle of smoke – and widely separated, with more than 320ft between particles.

- Statistically, UFO sightings are at their greatest number during those times when Mars is closest to the Earth.

- In the constellation Cygnus, there is a double star, one of whose components has such a high surface gravity that light cannot escape from it. Many

USELESS FACTS ABOUT THE UNIVERSE

astronomers believe Cygnus X-1 was the first 'black hole' to be detected.

- Temperature variations on Mercury are the most extreme in the solar system, ranging from 90K to 700K.

- In the 16th and 17th centuries, some people thought comets were the eggs or sperm of planetary systems.

- Barnard's star is approaching the Sun at a speed of 87 miles per second. By the year 11800 it will be the closest star to us.

- Because it is pouring energy out into space so rapidly, the Sun is shedding weight equivalent to that of a million elephants every second.

- Because of the speed at which the Earth moves around the Sun, it is impossible for a solar eclipse to last more than 7 minutes and 58 seconds.

- The entire planet of Saturn would float in water as it is made up mainly of gas.

- The Andromeda galaxy is the most distant object visible to the naked eye. It is about 12 billion billion miles away.

—USELESS FACTS ABOUT THE UNIVERSE—

- The Andromeda galaxy is the largest member of our local group of galaxies. The Milky Way is second largest in this group.

- Besides the Earth, only Jupiter, Saturn, Uranus and Neptune have known magnetic fields.

- By the year 14000 AD, the new North Star will be Vega.

- Carbon dioxide makes up 97% of Venus's atmosphere.

- Comets speed up as they approach the Sun – sometimes reaching speeds of over 1 million miles per hour. Far away from the Sun, speeds drop, perhaps down to as little as 700mph.

- The Earth orbits the Sun at 18.5 miles a second.

- The atmosphere of Mars is relatively moist. However, because the atmosphere is thin, the total amount of water in the atmosphere is minimal. If all the water in the atmosphere of Mars was collected, it would probably only fill a small pond.

- The average meteor, though brilliantly visible in the night-time sky, is no larger than a grain of sand. Even the largest and brightest meteors, known as fireballs, rarely exceed the size of a pea.

The Most Amazing Book of Useless Information of Them All

—USELESS FACTS ABOUT THE UNIVERSE—

- In the history of the solar system, 30 billion comets have been lost or destroyed. That amounts to only 30% of the estimated number that remain.

- In the Middle Ages, millions of people believed that the stars were beams of light shining through the floor of heaven.

- The average surface temperature of the outer planets – Uranus, Neptune, Pluto – is about -364°F, 11 times colder than inside a home freezer.

- It has been estimated that at least a million meteors have hit the Earth's land surface, which is only 25% of the planet. Every last trace of more than 99% of the craters thus formed has vanished, erased by wind, water and living things.

- The brightest asteroid is called Vesta. It has a diameter of 335 miles and is the only asteroid visible to the unaided eye.

- It is estimated by scientists that the universe contains 0.00000000000000000000000000001 grams of matter per cubic centimetre of space. It is also estimated that the universe is 35 billion light-years in size, or 210,000,000,000,000,000,000,000 miles.

- Deimos, one of Mars's moons, rises and sets twice a day.

—USELESS FACTS ABOUT THE UNIVERSE—

- It is estimated that, within the entire universe, there are more than a trillion galaxies.

- The brightness of a star is called its magnitude. The smaller the magnitude, the brighter the star.

- American physicist John Wheeler discovered the black holes of outer space, and he named the phenomenon in 1967.

- The coldest place in the solar system is the surface of Neptune's largest moon Triton, which has a temperature of -391°F, only 69°F above absolute zero.

- It takes 100,000 years for a red giant to change into a white dwarf. By astronomical standards, this is practically instantaneous, a mere one-thousandth of the star's life.

- The dark spots on the moon that create the benevolent 'man in the moon' image are actually basins filled 3–8km deep with basalt, a dense mineral, which causes immense gravitation variations.

- Jupiter is the largest planet, and it has the shortest day. Although Jupiter has a circumference of 280,000 miles, compared with the Earth's 25,000 miles, Jupiter manages to make one turn in 9 hours and 55 minutes. However, its years are 12 times as long as the Earth's.

—USELESS FACTS ABOUT THE UNIVERSE—

- Jupiter is so big and has such a large atmosphere that many astronomers think it almost became a star.

- The Sun is nearly 600 times bigger than all the planets combined.

- The Sun isn't round. It is flattened on the top and the bottom.

- The Sun is so far from Neptune – 2,793,000,000 miles – that from there it would appear to be no more than a very bright star.

- The dense globules of gas from which stars are born are much larger than the stars they will form. In the Orion nebula, globules have been detected which are 500 times larger than the solar system.

- The Sun produces more energy every minute than all the energy used on Earth in a whole year.

- The diameter of the star Betelgeuse is more than a quarter the size of our entire solar system.

- Every day the Sun provides our planet with 126,000,000,000,000 horsepower of energy. This means that 54,000 horsepower is delivered to every man, woman and child on Earth in each 24-hour period.

USELESS FACTS ABOUT THE UNIVERSE

- The distance around the Earth's equator is 24,920 miles; it would take 33,000,000 people holding hands to reach across that distance.

- The diameter of Venus is only about 400 miles less than that of the Earth.

- The Sun's equator is 2,717,952 miles around; it would take 3,645,000,000 people holding hands to go around it.

- Jupiter spins faster than any other planet. A point on the equator of Jupiter spins faster around the centre of the planet at a speed of 28,273mph. The speed of the spin makes the planet bulge slightly at its equator.

- The Sun's solar wind is so powerful it has large effects on the tails of comets, and scientists have determined that it even has measurable effects on the trajectories of spacecraft.

- The Sun's surface area is 12,000 times that of the Earth.

- The Earth's Moon has no global magnetic field.

- The Sun's total lifetime as a star capable of maintaining a life-bearing Earth is about 11 billion years, nearly half of which has passed.

USELESS FACTS ABOUT THE UNIVERSE

- Jupiter's moon Adrastea is one of the smallest moons in our solar system. It measures about 20km (12.4 miles).

- The Earth moves in its 585-million-mile orbit around the Sun approximately 8 times faster than a bullet travels.

- Just 20 seconds' worth of fuel remained when Apollo 11's lunar module landed on the moon.

- The Earth rotates on its axis more slowly in March than it does in September.

- Even though there were only 6 manned lunar landings, there are 7 Apollo lunar landers on the moon. Apollo X, as part of their mission, dropped their lunar lander to test seismic equipment that had already been set up on a previous mission.

- Five times as many meteors can be seen after midnight as can seen before.

- Four million tons of hydrogen dust are destroyed on the Sun every second.

- Because of its surface tension, free-moving liquid in outer space will form itself into a sphere.

—USELESS FACTS ABOUT THE UNIVERSE—

- Galaxies come in many different shapes, which are determined by the effects of past gravitational encounters with other galaxies. Our Milky Way is a spiral-type galaxy.

- Neptune has 8 known satellites.

- The surface of Venus is actually hotter than Mercury's, despite being nearly twice as far from the Sun.

- The Earth weighs nearly 6,588,000,000,000,000,000,000,000 tons.

- The surface temperature of a neutron star is about 1.8 million degrees Fahrenheit.

- The energy released in 1 hour by a single sunspot is equal to all the electrical power that will be used in the USA over the next million years.

- The surface of Venus – millions of miles away and hidden by clouds of sulphuric acid – has been better mapped than the Earth's seabed.

- The tail of a comet can extend 90 million miles – nearly the distance between the Earth and the Sun.

- The final resting place for Dr Eugene Shoemaker is the Moon. The famed US Geological Survey

USELESS FACTS ABOUT THE UNIVERSE

astronomer had trained the Apollo mission astronauts about craters, but never made it into space. Dr Shoemaker had wanted to be an astronaut but was rejected because of a medical problem. His ashes were placed on board the Lunar Prospector spacecraft before it was launched on 6 January 1998. NASA crashed the probe into a crater on the moon on 31 July 1999 in an attempt to learn if there is water on the Moon.

- Less than 50% of American adults understand that the Earth orbits the Sun yearly, according to a basic science survey.

- The tails of comets generally point away from the Sun whether the comet is approaching the Sun or whether it is receding.

- The first photo of the Earth taken from space was shot from the Vanguard 2 in 1959.

- Light takes one-tenth of a second to travel from New York to London, 8 minutes to reach the Earth from the Sun and 4.3 years to reach the Earth from the nearest star.

- The Tarantula is the largest known nebula. It is 160,000 light-years away. If it was as close to us as the Orion nebula, its light would cast shadows on Earth.

USELESS FACTS ABOUT THE UNIVERSE

- The first pulsar (a celestial object that emits brief, sharp pulses of radio waves instead of the steady radiation associated with other natural sources), discovered in 1967, never varies in its timing by even as much as a hundred-millionth of a second. Its pulse is registered every 1.33730109 seconds.

- Light from the Moon takes about a second and a half to reach the Earth.

- The Tarantula nebula is thought to contain a huge star of over 1,000 times the mass of the Sun, 10 times more massive than any star in the Milky Way.

- The first spacecraft to send back pictures of the far side of the Moon was Luna 3 in October 1959. The photographs covered about 70% of the far side.

- Liquid water was found inside a 4.5-billion-year-old meteorite in 1999, giving scientists their first look at extraterrestrial water.

- The telescope on Mount Palomar, California, can see a distance of 7,038,835,200,000,000,000,000 miles.

- The force of gravity is very strong on a neutron star because of its amazing density. Your weight on a neutron star would be 10,000 million times greater than on Earth.

USELESS FACTS ABOUT THE UNIVERSE

- The temperature of the Earth's interior increases by 1 degree every 60ft down.

- The temperature on the Moon reaches 243°F at midday on the lunar equator. During the night, the temperature falls to -261°F.

- The footprints left by the Apollo astronauts will not erode since there is no wind or water on the Moon and they should last at least 10 million years.

- Mare Tranquillitatis, or Sea of Tranquillity, was the name of the first manned lunar landing.

- Galileo became totally blind shortly before his death, probably because of the damage done to his eyes during his many years of looking at the Sun through a telescope.

- Halley's Comet is named after Edmond G Halley, who was the first to suggest that comets were natural phenomena of our solar system, in orbit around the Sun.

- Maps showing the solar system published prior to 1979 needed to be updated as Pluto was no longer the most distant planet from the Sun and it was Neptune instead. In its 248.8-year orbital revolution around the Sun, Pluto crossed Neptune's orbit in

—USELESS FACTS ABOUT THE UNIVERSE—

December 1978. Neptune and Pluto resumed their more familiar positions in March 1999 as Pluto journeyed to its farthest point from the Sun, over 4.5 billion miles away.

- Ganymede, Jupiter's largest moon, is bigger than Mercury, the smallest planet. It is 3,275 miles in diameter.

- Giant flames called prominences shoot out from the Sun's surfaces for 310,000 miles, more than the distance from the Earth to the Moon. The entire Earth could fit into one of these flames nearly 40 times.

- Mars takes 1.88 years to orbit the Sun, so its seasons are about twice as long as those on Earth.

- If a pin was heated to the same temperature as the centre of the Sun, its heat would set alight everything within 60 miles of it.

- If a red giant star was the size of an ordinary living room, its energy-generating core would be the size of the full stop at the end of this sentence.

- The giant red star Betelgeuse – the red star in the shoulder of the constellation Orion – is 700 million miles across, about 800 times larger than the Sun.

USELESS FACTS ABOUT THE UNIVERSE

Light takes one hour to travel from one side of the giant star to the other.

- The Veil nebula was formed by an explosion which took place over 30,000 years ago when the first people lived on Earth.

- If an astronaut tried to land on a neutron star, he or she would be crushed by the extremely strong force of gravity, and squashed into a thin layer less than 1 atom thick.

- The existence of Mercury has been known since about the third millennium BC. The planet was given two names by the Greeks: Apollo, for its apparition as a morning star, and Hermes as an evening star. Greek astronomers knew, however, that the two names referred to the same body.

- The universe is about 15,000 million years old. Put another way, if the years flashed by at a rate of 1 each second, the universe would already be nearly 47 years old.

- Halley's Comet, one of the most famous comets, returns to Earth every 76 years, and has been observed and recorded for more than 3,000 years.

- The winds of Venus blow steadily at 109mph.

—USELESS FACTS ABOUT THE UNIVERSE—

- Metis is the innermost of Jupiter's known satellites and was named after Metis, a Titaness who was the first wife of the Greek god Zeus, known later as Jupiter in Roman mythology.

- The gravitational pull of a black hole is so strong that, if a 2-pound book were brought within 20ft of a black hole, the book would weigh more than all the world's population combined.

- Millions of meteorites fall against the outer limits of the atmosphere every day and are burned to nothing by the friction.

- The Venus day is longer than the Venus year. The planet spins on its axis once every 243 Earth days and orbits the Sun once every 224 Earth days.

- The Great Red Spot on Jupiter is a swirling hurricane of gases. The winds in the hurricane reach 21,700mph.

- More than 100,000 asteroids lie in a belt between Mars and Jupiter.

- The weight of the Sun is 2 billion billion billion tons, about 333,420 times that of the Earth.

- The word comet comes from the Greek kométes, meaning 'wearing long hair'.

—USELESS FACTS ABOUT THE UNIVERSE—

- The heaviest known meteorite to fall to Earth – the Hoba West meteorite – lies where it fell in Africa. Weighing about 60 tons, it is not likely to be moved.

- More than 20 million meteroids enter the Earth's atmosphere every day, but most are no bigger than a speck of dust.

- The Hercules global cluster is the brightest cluster in the northern sky. It was discovered by English scientist Edmond Halley in 1714.

- The Hubble Space Telescope recently discovered a huge 295-mile crater on the asteroid Vesta. This is massive when compared to Vesta's 330-mile diameter. If the Earth had a crater of proportional size, it would fill most of the Pacific Ocean basin.

- The world is not round. It is an oblate spheroid, flattened at the poles and bulging at the equator.

- The huge halo of comets that surrounds our solar system is called the Oort Cloud.

- Neil Armstrong's spacesuit during his training brought in $178,500 at auction. This was more than double its pre-sale estimate.

- The jets of water vapour discharged by a comet have a

—USELESS FACTS ABOUT THE UNIVERSE—

rocket-like effect. They alter the comet's orbit enough to make its course unpredictable.

- Neptune is a maximum distance of 2.82 billion miles from the Sun. The length of one of its days is 17 hours 6 minutes and the length of one of its years is 165 Earth days.

- Eighty-eight different constellations have been identified and named by astronomers.

- There are 7 rings surrounding Saturn. Each of the rings is made up of thousands of ringlets, which are made up of billions of objects of varying sizes from 33ft-wide icebergs to pinhead-small ice specks.

- The largest crater that can be seen on the Moon is called Bailly, or the 'fields of ruin'. It covers an area of about 26,000 square miles, about three times the size of Wales.

- There is a correspondence between the fluctuation of agricultural production and sunspot variations. Production of wheat, for example, reached high figures during sunspot maximums and low figures during sunspot minimums.

- There is now evidence that comets are propelled into the inner solar system by the tidal pull of the entire

USELESS FACTS ABOUT THE UNIVERSE

galaxy, rather than by the pull of passing stars, as many astronomers had believed. And, just as the Moon pulls the Earth's oceans upwards on a regular, predictable timetable, the galaxy's pull on comets also follows a predictable pattern, causing greatly increased comet activity about once every 35 million years.

- The largest refracting telescope is the 40in Yerkes telescope, built in 1897 and still in use. All larger telescopes are of the 'reflecting' variety, using mirrors instead of lenses.

- Neptune is so remote that light from the Sun – though travelling at 186,000 miles per second – takes more than 4 hours to reach the planet. By comparison, light from the Sun takes only 8 minutes to reach the Earth.

- The Moon weighs 81 billion tons.

- The largest volcano known is on Mars: Olympus Mons, 370 miles wide and 79,000ft high, is almost three times higher than Mount Everest.

- Three-quarters of the galaxies in the universe are spiral galaxies. There are three other types of galaxies: elliptical, irregular and lenticular.

- Venus is much brighter than any other planet or star.

USELESS FACTS ABOUT THE UNIVERSE

- There may be a giant black hole at the centre of our galaxy, weighing as much as 4 million Suns. The black hole may be capturing stars, gas and dust equivalent to the weight of three Earths every year.

- The layer of gas that spreads out from a nova explosion can be travelling at speeds of 5 million miles per hour.

- On 21 September 1978 two Soviet cosmonauts set a space endurance record of 96 days.

- Time slows down near a black hole; inside, it stops completely.

- The Moon is 238,330 miles away from the Earth. At that distance, the Moon is the Earth's closest neighbour.

- The Moon is about as wide as the United States: 2,160 miles.

- On Venus, the Sun rises in the West and sets in the East, the opposite of the Earth. Venus rotates from East to West, not from West to East as the Earth and the other planets do.

- Titan, Saturn's largest moon, is the only moon in our solar system to have an atmosphere. However, it

USELESS FACTS ABOUT THE UNIVERSE

cannot support life as its atmosphere is made of nitrogen and methane gas.

- The Moon is one million times drier than the Gobi Desert.

- The Moon is always falling. It has a sideways motion of its own that balances its falling motion. It therefore stays in a closed orbit about the Earth, never falling altogether and never escaping altogether.

- One day on Mercury lasts for 176 Earth days. The big time difference is due to Mercury's length of rotation, which is much slower than the Earth's.

- To an observer standing on Pluto, the Sun would appear no brighter than Venus appears in our evening sky.

- Travelling at the speed of 186,000 miles per second, light takes 6 hours to travel from Pluto to the Earth.

- Triton, a moon of Neptune, is the coldest known place in the solar system. Its surface is 390°F below zero.

- The most ancient report of a solar eclipse is in Chinese records. According to legend, the eclipse came without warning because the royal astronomers, Hsi and Ho, were too drunk to make the necessary

USELESS FACTS ABOUT THE UNIVERSE

computations. They were executed – the only astronomers known to have been killed for dereliction of duty.

- The largest number of telescopes in one city in the world is in Tucson, Arizona.

- The moons of Mars are called Phobos and Deimos after two mythical horses that drew the chariot of Mars, the Roman God of War.

- Until the mid-sixteenth century, comets were believed to be not astronomical phenomena, but burning vapours that had arisen from distant swamps and were propelled across the sky by fire and light.

- Our galaxy probably contains millions of old neutron stars that have stopped spinning, and so are undetectable.

- Our solar system lies halfway along the Orion arm, about 24,000 light-years from the galactic centre.

- Venus has no magnetic field, perhaps because of its slow rotation. It also has no satellites.

- The most luminous star is probably Eta Carinae, which has a maximum luminosity of around 5 million times that of the Sun.

—USELESS FACTS ABOUT THE UNIVERSE—

- Our Sun burns 9 million tons of gas a second. At this rate, it has been estimated that it will burn out in another 10 billion years.

- Plenilune is an archaic term for a full moon.

- The multi-layered space suit worn by astronauts on the Apollo moon landings weighed 180lb on Earth and 30lb on the Moon with the reduced lunar gravity.

- Phobos, one of the moons of Mars, is so close to its parent planet that it could not be seen by an observer standing at either of Mars's poles. Every day Phobos makes three complete orbits around Mars.

- When astronauts first shaved in space, their weightless whiskers floated up to the ceiling. A special razor had to be developed, which drew the whiskers in like a vacuum cleaner.

- Physicists now believe the universe to be 3 billion years younger than previously thought. New information gathered by the Hipparcos satellite, combined with a re-analysis of other distance data, has enabled researchers to refine the lower age limit of the universe to 9.6 billion years.

- When the first pulsar signal was detected in 1967, it was thought that its signals might be a message from

—USELESS FACTS ABOUT THE UNIVERSE—

an alien civilisation deep in space. The signal was jokingly labelled 'LGM', for 'little green men'.

- At its brightest, the Moon can cast shadow, and can even be seen during the daytime.

- The nucleus of Halley's Comet is a peanut-shaped object, weighing about 100,000 million tons, and measuring about 9 x 5 miles.

- Venus, the Earth's nearest planetary neighbour, at its closest to us, is 105 times farther away than our Moon.

- Proxima Centauri is the closest star to the Earth (outside our solar system), but it is too small to be seen without a telescope.

- Pluto's one moon, Charon, is 12,200 miles from the planet and has a diameter of just 740 miles. First seen from the Earth in 1978, tiny Charon is similar in size to Pluto. The two bodies orbit each other like a double planet, with the same sides permanently facing each other. Pluto and Charon are so close in proximity it is believed that they may share an atmosphere.

- Polaris, in the tail of the Little Bear constellation, is the closest visible star to true north and thus is referred to as the North Star. By about 2100, the

USELESS FACTS ABOUT THE UNIVERSE

wobble of the Earth's axis will slowly begin pointing the North Pole away from Polaris.

- The oldest features on Venus appear to be no older than 800 million years.

- Jupiter has 16 moons, the largest of which is Ganymede, which looks like cracked eggshell.

- When the Apollo 12 astronauts landed on the Moon, the impact caused the Moon's surface to vibrate for 55 minutes. The vibrations were picked up by laboratory instruments, leading geologists to theorise that the Moon's surface is composed of fragile layers of rock.

- Uranus has 15 known satellites.

- Jupiter is named after the supreme god of the Romans. He was the God of the Sky, the bringer of light, hurling lightning bolts down on the world when displeased.

- Quasars are amazingly bright objects. A quasar generates 100 times as much light as the whole of our galaxy in a space not much larger than our solar system.

- When we look at the farthest visible star, we are looking 4 billion years into the past – the light from

—USELESS FACTS ABOUT THE UNIVERSE—

that star, travelling at 186,000 miles a second, has taken that many years to reach us.

- Winds 10 times stronger than a hurricane on Earth blow around Saturn's equator. Wind speeds can reach 1,100mph.

- Pluto takes 248 Earth years to orbit the Sun. For 20 of those years, it is closer to the Sun than Neptune. The nature of its orbit, however, always prevents it from colliding with Neptune.

- Scientists are still finding new planets, but not in our solar system. Recently, a new planet was discovered orbiting the star Epsilon Eridani, which is only 10.5 light-years from the Earth.

- Saturn would float on water if there was an ocean large enough to accommodate it because of its density. However, Saturn is 95 times heavier than the Earth.

14

SAYINGS OF OSCAR WILDE, 1854-1900

SAYINGS OF OSCAR WILDE, 1854-1900

- 'It is a very sad thing that nowadays there is so little useless information.'

- 'A cynic is a man who knows the price of everything but the value of nothing. A gentleman is one who never hurts anyone's feelings unintentionally.'

- 'A little sincerity is a dangerous thing, and a great deal of it is absolutely fatal.'

- 'A man can't be too careful in the choice of his enemies.'

- 'A man's face is his autobiography. A woman's face is her work of fiction.'

- 'A poet can survive everything but a misprint.'

- 'A thing is not necessarily true because a man dies for it.'

- 'A true friend stabs you in the front.'

- 'A work of art is the unique result of a unique temperament.'

- 'Women are made to be loved, not understood.'

- 'Alas, I am dying beyond my means.'

SAYINGS OF OSCAR WILDE, 1854-1900

- 'All bad poetry springs from genuine feeling.'

- 'All that I desire to point out is the general principle that life imitates art far more than art imitates life.'

- 'All women become like their mothers. That is their tragedy. No man does. That's his.'

- 'Work is the curse of the drinking classes.'

- 'Always forgive your enemies – nothing annoys them so much.'

- 'Ambition is the germ from which all growth of nobleness proceeds.'

- 'Ambition is the last refuge of the failure.'

- 'America is the only country that went from barbarism to decadence without civilisation in between.'

- 'An idea that is not dangerous is unworthy of being called an idea at all.'

- 'Arguments are extremely vulgar, for everyone in good society holds exactly the same opinion.'

- 'Arguments are to be avoided: they are always vulgar and often convincing.'

—— SAYINGS OF OSCAR WILDE, 1854-1900 ——

- 'When the gods wish to punish us they answer our prayers.'

- 'As long as a woman can look ten years younger than her own daughter, she is perfectly satisfied.'

- 'As long as war is regarded as wicked, it will always have its fascination. When it is looked upon as vulgar, it will cease to be popular.'

- 'As yet, Bernard Shaw hasn't become prominent enough to have any enemies, but none of his friends like him.'

- 'At 46, one must be a miser; only have time for essentials.'

- 'Bigamy is having one wife too many. Monogamy is the same.'

- 'Yet each man kills the thing he loves, by each let this be heard, some do it with a bitter look, some with a flattering word. The coward does it with a kiss, the brave man with a sword!'

- 'Children begin by loving their parents; after a time they judge them; rarely, if ever, do they forgive them.'

- 'Biography lends to death a new terror.'

SAYINGS OF OSCAR WILDE, 1854-1900

- 'Between men and women there is no friendship possible. There is passion, enmity, worship, love, but no friendship.'

- 'Between the optimist and the pessimist, the difference is droll. The optimist sees the doughnut; the pessimist the hole!'

- 'Charity creates a multitude of sins.'

- 'Why was I born with such contemporaries?'

- 'Woman begins by resisting a man's advances and ends by blocking his retreat.'

- 'Conscience and cowardice are really the same things. Conscience is the trade-name of the firm. That is all.'

- 'Conversation about the weather is the last refuge of the unimaginative.'

- 'Deceiving others. That is what the world calls a romance.'

- 'Whenever people agree with me I always feel I must be wrong.'

- 'Democracy means simply the bludgeoning of the people by the people for the people.'

SAYINGS OF OSCAR WILDE, 1854-1900

- 'Do you really think it is weakness that yields to temptation? I tell you that there are terrible temptations which it requires strength, strength and courage to yield to.'

- 'Each class preaches the importance of those virtues it need not exercise. The rich harp on the value of thrift, the idle grow eloquent over the dignity of labour.'

- 'Education is an admirable thing, but it is well to remember from time to time that nothing that is worth knowing can be taught.'

- 'Every portrait that is painted with feeling is a portrait of the artist, not of the sitter.'

- 'Every saint has a past and every sinner has a future.'

- 'When good Americans die they go to Paris.'

- 'When I was young I thought that money was the most important thing in life; now that I am old I know that it is.'

- 'Experience is simply the name we give our mistakes.'

- 'Hatred is blind, as well as love. He hadn't a single redeeming vice. He has no enemies, but is intensely disliked by his friends. He lives the poetry that he

SAYINGS OF OSCAR WILDE, 1854-1900

cannot write. The others write the poetry that they dare not realise. He must have a truly romantic nature, for he weeps when there is nothing at all to weep about. He was always late on principle, his principle being that punctuality is the thief of time.'

- 'Fashion is a form of ugliness so intolerable that we have to alter it every six months.'

- 'Fathers should be neither seen nor heard. That is the only proper basis for family life.'

- 'How can a woman be expected to be happy with a man who insists on treating her as if she were a perfectly normal human being?'

- 'How marriage ruins a man! It is as demoralising as cigarettes, and far more expensive.'

- 'How strange a thing this is! The Priest telleth me that the Soul is worth all the gold in the world, and the merchants say that it is not worth a clipped piece of silver.'

- 'I always pass on good advice. It is the only thing to do with it. It is never of any use to oneself.'

- 'I never travel without my diary. One should always have something sensational to read in the train.'

SAYINGS OF OSCAR WILDE, 1854-1900

- 'I am not young enough to know everything.'

- 'I can resist everything except temptation. I choose my friends for their good looks, my acquaintances for their good characters, and my enemies for their intellects.'

- 'I have nothing to declare except my genius. I have the simplest tastes. I am always satisfied with the best. I hope you have not been leading a double life, pretending to be wicked and being really good all the time. That would be hypocrisy.'

- 'I put all my genius into my life; I put only my talent into my works.'

- 'When a woman marries again it is because she detested her first husband. When a man marries again, it is because he adored his first wife. Women try their luck; men risk theirs.'

- 'I see when men love women. They give them but a little of their lives. But women when they love give everything.'

- 'I sometimes think that God in creating man somewhat overestimated his ability.'

- 'If one cannot enjoy reading a book over and over again, there is no use in reading it at all.'

SAYINGS OF OSCAR WILDE, 1854-1900

- 'I suppose society is wonderfully delightful. To be in it is merely a bore. But to be out of it is simply a tragedy.'

- 'I want my food dead. Not sick, not dying, dead.'

- 'If one could only teach the English how to talk, and the Irish how to listen, society here would be quite civilised.'

- 'If one plays good music, people don't listen and if one plays bad music, people don't talk.'

- 'If there was less sympathy in the world, there would be less trouble in the world.'

- 'If you are not too long, I will wait here for you all my life.'

- 'What we have to do, what at any rate it is our duty to do, is to revive the old art of Lying.'

- 'If you pretend to be good, the world takes you very seriously. If you pretend to be bad, it doesn't. Such is the astounding stupidity of optimism.'

- 'In America the young are always ready to give to those who are older than themselves the full benefits of their inexperience.'

— SAYINGS OF OSCAR WILDE, 1854-1900 —

- 'In America the President reigns for four years, and Journalism governs forever and ever.'

- 'In all matters of opinion, our adversaries are insane.'

- 'In England people actually try to be brilliant at breakfast. That is so dreadful of them! Only dull people are brilliant at breakfast.'

- 'In every first novel the hero is the author as Christ or Faust.'

- 'It is absurd to divide people into good and bad. People are either charming or tedious.'

- 'It is an odd thing, but everyone who disappears is said to be seen at San Francisco. It must be a delightful city, and possess all the attractions of the next world.'

- 'It is better to be beautiful than to be good. But... it is better to be good than to be ugly.'

- 'Its failings notwithstanding, there is much to be said in favour of journalism in that, by giving us the opinion of the uneducated, it keeps us in touch with the ignorance of the community.'

- 'It is better to have a permanent income than to be fascinating.'

SAYINGS OF OSCAR WILDE, 1854-1900

- 'In married life three is company and two none.'

- 'Illusion is the first of all pleasures.'

- 'It is only an auctioneer who can equally and impartially admire all schools of art.'

- 'It is through art, and through art only, that we can realise our perfection.'

- 'It is perfectly monstrous the way people go about, nowadays, saying things against one behind one's back that are absolutely and entirely true.'

- 'Women are never disarmed by compliments. Men always are. That is the difference between the sexes.'

- 'Laughter is not at all a bad beginning for a friendship, and it is far the best ending for one.'

- 'Life is far too important a thing ever to talk seriously about.'

- 'Life is never fair, and perhaps it is a good thing for most of us that it is not.'

- 'When a man has once loved a woman he will do anything for her except continue to love her.'

SAYINGS OF OSCAR WILDE, 1854-1900

- 'Man is least himself when he talks in his own person. Give him a mask, and he will tell you the truth.'

- 'Memory... is the diary that we all carry about with us.'

- 'Men always want to be a woman's first love – women like to be a man's last romance.'

- 'Mere colour, unspoiled by meaning, and unallied with definite form, can speak to the soul in a thousand different ways.'

- 'Moderation is a fatal thing. Nothing succeeds like excess.'

- 'Morality is simply the attitude we adopt towards people whom we personally dislike.'

- 'Most modern calendars mar the sweet simplicity of our lives by reminding us that each day that passes is the anniversary of some perfectly uninteresting event.'

- 'Most people are other people. Their thoughts are someone else's opinions, their lives a mimicry, their passions a quotation.'

- 'Most people die of a sort of creeping common sense, and discover when it is too late that the only things one never regrets are one's mistakes.'

SAYINGS OF OSCAR WILDE, 1854-1900

- 'Nothing is so aggravating than calmness.'

- 'No woman should ever be quite accurate about her age. It looks so calculating.'

- 'No man is rich enough to buy back his past.'

- 'Music makes one feel so romantic – at least it always gets on one's nerves – which is the same thing nowadays.'

- 'My great mistake, the fault for which I can't forgive myself, is that one day I ceased my obstinate pursuit of my own individuality.'

- 'No great artist ever sees things as they really are. If he did, he would cease to be an artist.'

- 'No object is so beautiful that, under certain conditions, it will not look ugly.'

- 'Now that the House of Commons is trying to become useful, it does a great deal of harm.'

- 'Nowadays to be intelligible is to be found out.'

- 'Of course America had often been discovered before Columbus, but it had always been hushed up.'

SAYINGS OF OSCAR WILDE, 1854–1900

- 'Of course I have played outdoor games. I once played dominoes in an open-air cafe in Paris.'

- 'One of the many lessons that one learns in prison is that things are what they are and will be what they will be.'

- 'One can survive everything, nowadays, except death, and live down everything except a good reputation.'

- 'One should always be in love. That is the reason one should never marry.'

- 'One should always play fairly when one has the winning cards.'

- 'One's past is what one is. It is the only way by which people should be judged.'

- 'We are all in the gutter, but some of us are looking at the stars.'

- 'Only the shallow know themselves.'

- 'Ordinary riches can be stolen; real riches cannot. In your soul are infinitely precious things that cannot be taken from you.'

- 'Patriotism is the virtue of the vicious.'

SAYINGS OF OSCAR WILDE, 1854-1900

- 'Self-denial is the shining sore on the leprous body of Christianity.'

- 'Our ambition should be to rule ourselves, the true kingdom for each one of us; and true progress is to know more, and be more, and to do more.'

- 'Perhaps, after all, America never has been discovered. I myself would say that it had merely been detected.'

- 'Pessimist: One who, when he has the choice of two evils, chooses both.'

- 'Questions are never indiscreet, answers sometimes are.'

- 'Relations are simply a tedious pack of people, who haven't got the remotest knowledge of how to live, nor the smallest instinct about when to die.'

- 'Selfishness is not living as one wishes to live, it is asking others to live as one wishes to live.'

- 'Seriousness is the only refuge of the shallow.'

- 'She wore far too much rouge last night and not quite enough clothes. That is always a sign of despair in a woman.'

- 'The basis of optimism is sheer terror.'

SAYINGS OF OSCAR WILDE, 1854-1900

- 'Some cause happiness wherever they go; others whenever they go.'

- 'Some of these people need ten years of therapy – ten sentences of mine do not equal ten years of therapy.'

- 'Success is a science; if you have the conditions, you get the result.'

- 'The books that the world calls immoral are books that show the world its own shame.'

- 'The difference between literature and journalism is that journalism is unreadable and literature is not read.'

- 'The English country gentleman galloping after a fox: The unspeakable in full pursuit of the uneatable.'

- 'The imagination imitates. It is the critical spirit that creates.'

- 'The liar at any rate recognises that recreation, not instruction, is the aim of conversation, and is a far more civilised being than the blockhead who loudly expresses his disbelief in a story which is told simply for the amusement of the company.'

- 'The man who can dominate a London dinner table can dominate the world.'

SAYINGS OF OSCAR WILDE, 1854-1900

- 'The moment you think you understand a great work of art, it's dead for you.'

- 'The old believe everything, the middle-aged suspect everything, the young know everything.'

- 'The one charm about marriage is that it makes a life of deception absolutely necessary for both parties.'

- 'The past is of no importance. The present is of no importance. It is with the future that we have to deal. For the past is what man should not have been. The present is what man ought not to be. The future is what artists are.'

- 'The public have an insatiable curiosity to know everything. Except what is worth knowing. Journalism, conscious of this, and having tradesman-like habits, supplies their demands.'

- 'The public is wonderfully tolerant. It forgives everything except genius.'

- 'The pure and simple truth is rarely pure and never simple.'

- 'The salesman knows nothing of what he is selling save that he is charging a great deal too much for it.'

SAYINGS OF OSCAR WILDE, 1854-1900

- 'The typewriting machine, when played with expression, is no more annoying than the piano when played by a sister or near relation.'

- 'The true mystery of the world is the visible, not the invisible.'

- 'The security of Society lies in custom and unconscious instinct, and the basis of the stability of Society, as a healthy organism, is the complete absence of any intelligence amongst its members.'

- 'The world has grown suspicious of anything that looks like a happily married life.'

- 'The world is divided into two classes, those who believe the incredible, and those who do the improbable.'

- 'There are only two kinds of people who are really fascinating – people who know absolutely everything, and people who know absolutely nothing. There are only two tragedies in life: one is not getting what one wants, and the other is getting it.'

- 'There are two ways of disliking poetry; one way is to dislike it, the other is to read Pope.'

- 'This suspense is terrible. I hope it will last.'

SAYINGS OF OSCAR WILDE, 1854-1900

- 'There is no such thing as a moral or an immoral book. Books are well written, or badly written.'

- 'To expect the unexpected shows a thoroughly modern intellect.'

- 'There is no such thing as an omen. Destiny does not send us heralds. She is too wise or too cruel for that.'

- 'To lose one parent may be regarded as a misfortune; to lose both looks like carelessness.'

- 'They afterwards took me to a dancing saloon where I saw the only rational method of art criticism I have ever come across. Over the piano was printed a notice "Please do not shoot the pianist. He is doing his best."'

- 'Those whom the gods love grow young.'

- 'There is no sin except stupidity.'

15
Usless Facts about Geography

USLESS FACTS ABOUT GEOGRAPHY

- The shortest place names in the USA are 'L', a lake in Nebraska, 'T', a gulch in Colorado, 'D', a river in Oregon flowing from Devil's Lake to the Ocean, and 'Y', a city in Arkansas, each named after its shape.

- In Europe, 'E' is a river in Perthshire, Scotland; there are villages called 'Å' in Norway, Sweden and Denmark, and a 'Y' in France.

- The Pacific Caroline Islands has a place named 'U' and a peak in Hong Kong is called 'A'.

- Benjamin Franklin was first to suggest daylight saving.

- The most abundant metal in the Earth's crust is aluminium.

- It snowed in the Sahara Desert on 18 February 1979.

- Captain Cook was the first man to set foot on all continents except Antarctica.

- 200 million years ago, the Earth contained one land mass called Pangaea.

- It is illegal to swim in Central Park, New York.

- At the deepest point (11.034km), an iron ball would take more than an hour to sink to the ocean floor.

USLESS FACTS ABOUT GEOGRAPHY

- The largest wave ever recorded was near the Japanese Island of Ishigaki in 1971, at 85m high.

- Antarctic means 'opposite the Artic'.

- The largest iceberg recorded, in 1956, was 200 miles long and 60 miles wide, larger than the country of Belgium.

- The surface of the Dead Sea is 400m below the surface of the Mediterranean Sea, which is only 75km away.

- The country of Benin changed its name from Dahomey in 1975.

- The Nova Zemlya Glacier in the former USSR is over 400km long.

- Canada (9,970,610 sq km) is larger than China (9,596,961 sq km) which is larger than the USA (9,363,130 sq km).

- The coldest temperature ever recorded was -70°C in Siberia.

- The second largest US state in the 1950s was California.

USLESS FACTS ABOUT GEOGRAPHY

- Maryland was named after Queen Henrietta Maria.

- The only country to register zero births in 1983 was the Vatican City.

- Florida first saw the cultivation of oranges in 1539.

- The world's largest National Park is Wood Buffalo National Park in Canada.

- The world's largest exporter of sugar is Cuba.

- There are no rivers in Saudi Arabia.

- England's Stonehenge is 1,500 years older than Rome's Colosseum.

- In 1896 Britain and Zanzibar were at war for 38 minutes.

- The Eskimo language has over 20 words to describe different kinds of snow.

- Numbering houses in London streets only began in 1764.

- More than 75% of all the countries in the world are north of the equator.

USLESS FACTS ABOUT GEOGRAPHY

- Less than 1% of the Caribbean Islands are inhabited.

- Fulgurite is formed when lightning strikes sand.

- Mountains are formed by a process called orogeny.

- Obsidian, used by American Indians for tools, weapons and ornaments, is dark volcanic glass.

- Eighty-two per cent of the workers on the Panama Canal suffered from malaria.

- In May 1948 Mount Ruapehu and Mount Ngauruhoe, both in New Zealand, erupted simultaneously.

- The Incas and the Aztecs were able to function without the wheel.

- The tree on the Lebanese flag is a Cedar.

- Tokyo was once called Edo.

- The Atlantic Ocean covers the world's longest mountain range.

- In 1825 Upper Peru became Bolivia.

- New York City contains 920km of shoreline.

USLESS FACTS ABOUT GEOGRAPHY

- There are 3 Great pyramids at Giza.

- The southwestern tip of the Isle of Man is called The Calf of Man.

- The world's largest Delta was created by the River Ganges.

- The Scottish city Edinburgh is nicknamed 'Auld Reekie' meaning 'Old Smoky'.

- The inhabitants of Papua New Guinea speak about 700 languages (including localised dialects, which are known to change from village to village), approximately 15% of the world's total.

- The world's first National Park was Yellowstone National Park.

- Sixty per cent of all US potato products originate in Idaho.

- The northernmost country claiming part of Antarctica is Norway.

- The 'DC' in Washington DC stands for District of Columbia.

- New York's Central Park opened in 1876.

USLESS FACTS ABOUT GEOGRAPHY

- The inhabitants of Monaco are known as Monegasques.

- The East Alligator River in Australia's Northern Territory was misnamed. It contains crocodiles, not alligators.

- France contains the greatest length of paved roads.

- The city of Istanbul straddles two separate continents, Europe and Asia.

- At the nearest point Russia and America are less than 4km apart.

- Rio de Janeiro translates to 'River of January'.

- The furthest point from any ocean is in China.

- The Tibetan mountain people use yak's milk as their form of currency.

- Spain literally means 'the land of rabbits'.

- Underneath the great icy plains of the Antarctic little pools of unfrozen water can sometimes be found.

- Ten per cent of the salt mined in the world each year is used to de-ice the roads in America.

USLESS FACTS ABOUT GEOGRAPHY

- The Spanish Inquisition once condemned the entire Netherlands to death for heresy.

- The River Nile has frozen over only twice in living memory – once in the ninth century, and then again in the eleventh century.

- The Angel Falls in Venezuela are nearly 20 times taller than Niagara Falls.

- Dirty snow melts quicker than clean snow.

- The Scandinavian capital, Stockholm, is built on 9 islands connected by bridges.

- La Paz in Bolivia is so high above sea level that there is barely enough oxygen in the air to support a fire.

- The Forth railway bridge in Scotland is a metre longer in summer than in winter, due to thermal expansion.

- In the Andes, time is often measured by how long it takes to smoke a cigarette.

- Until the eighteenth century, India produced almost all the world's diamonds.

- The Earth's magnetic field is not permanent.

USLESS FACTS ABOUT GEOGRAPHY

- On 30 March 1867, Alaska was officially purchased from Russia for about 2 cents an acre. At the time, many politicians believed this purchase of 'wasteland to be a costly folly'.

- During winter, the skating rinks in Moscow cover more than 250,000 sq m of land.

- As the Pacific plate moves under its coast, the North Island of New Zealand is getting larger.

- Brazil got its name from the nut, not the other way around.

- If you travel from East to West across the Soviet Union, you will cross 7 time zones.

- Sahara means 'desert' in Arabic.

- On 15 January 1867, there was a severe frost in London, and over 40 people died in Regent's Park when the ice broke on the main lake.

- The water in the Dead Seas is so salty that is far easier to float than to drown.

- The State flag of Alaska was designed by a 13-year-old boy.

USLESS FACTS ABOUT GEOGRAPHY

- Lightning strikes the Earth about 200 times a second.

- Very hard rain would pour down at the rate of about 20mph.

- Discounting Australia, which is generally regarded as a continental land mass, the world's largest island is Greenland.

- No rain has ever been recorded falling in the Atacama Desert in Chile.

- The background radiation in Aberdeen is twice that of the rest of Great Britain.

- About 2 million hydrogen atoms would be required to cover the full stop at the end of this sentence.

- The southernmost tip of Africa is not the Cape of Good Hope, but Cape Agulhas.

- The Tower of London, during its lifetime, has served many purposes, including a zoo.

- Two minor earthquakes occur every minute somewhere in the world.

- In the north of Norway, the sun shines constantly for about 14 weeks each summer.

USLESS FACTS ABOUT GEOGRAPHY

- The Polynesian country of Niue is a 170 sq km limestone rock emerging 60m from the Pacific.

- Icelandic phone books are listed by the given name, not the surname.

- The United States, which accounts for 6% of the population of the world, consumes nearly 60% of the world's resources.

- The world's longest freshwater beach is located in Canada.

- Over the years, the Niagara Falls have moved more than 11km from their original site.

- The number of births in India each year is greater than the entire population of Australia.

- Yugoslavia is bordered by 7 other countries.

- Greenland – thus named to attract settlers – was discovered by Eric the Red in the tenth century.

- Within a few years of Columbus's discovery of America, the Spaniards had killed 1.5 million Indians.

- Hawaii officially became a part of the USA on 14 June 1900.

USLESS FACTS ABOUT GEOGRAPHY

- The fastest tectonic movement on Earth is 240mm per year, at the Tonga micro-plate near Samoa.

- If the population of China walked past you in single file, the line would never end because of the rate of reproduction.

- The Earth is actually pear shaped, the North Pole radius being 44mm longer than the South Pole radius.

- In 1908 the Moskva River in Russia rose 9m, flooding 100 streets and 2,500 houses.

- There is about 200 times more gold in the world's oceans than has been mined in our entire history.

- A quarter of Russia is covered by forest.

- There is a Rocking Stone in Cornwall which, though it weighs many tonnes, can be rocked with ease.

- South Africa produces two-thirds of the world's gold.

- The volume of water in the Amazon River is greater than the next 8 largest rivers in the world combined.

- There is no point in England more than 75 miles from the ocean.

USLESS FACTS ABOUT GEOGRAPHY

- England is smaller than New England.

- Nearly a quarter of the population of Poland was killed in World War II.

- The first city in the world to have a population of over one million was London.

- There is a town in West Virginia called Looneyville.

- One of the greatest natural disasters of recent centuries occurred when an earthquake hit Tangshan, China, killing three-quarters of a million people.

- New York was once New Amsterdam.

- On Picarn Island, it is a criminal offence to shout 'ship ahoy!' when there is, in fact, no ship in sight.

- The Dead Sea is, in fact, an inland lake.

- There are 6 million trees in the Forest of Martyrs near Jerusalem, symbolising the Jewish death toll in World War II.

- Hawaii's Mount Waialeale is the wettest place in the world – it rains about 90% of the time, about 480in per annum.

16
USELESS STATISTICS

USELESS STATISTICS

- At -40°C, a person loses about 14.4 calories per hour by breathing.

- One million Americans, about 3,000 each day, take up smoking each year. Most of them are children.

- In 1933 Mickey Mouse, an animated cartoon character, received 800,000 fan letters.

- If you attempted to count all the stars in a galaxy at a rate of 1 every second, it would take around 3,000 years to count them all.

- Less than 3% of Nestlé's sales are for chocolate.

- The average chocolate bar has 8 insects' legs in it.

- There are 2 credit cards for every person in the United States.

- The average person will spend 2 weeks over their lifetime waiting for the traffic light to change.

- More than 2,500 left-handed people are killed every year from using right-handed products.

- February 1865 and February 1999 are the only months in recorded history not to have a full moon.

USELESS STATISTICS

- The most common name in the world is Mohammed.

- More people are killed by donkeys annually than are killed in plane crashes.

- The only 2 days of the year in which there are no professional sports games in the USA (MLB, NBA, NHL or NFL) are the day before and the day after the Major League All-Star Game.

- Only one person in 2 billion will live to be 116 or older.

- You share your birthday with at least 9 million other people in the world.

- It is estimated that, at any one time, 0.7% of the world's population are drunk.

- The tip of a ⅓in-long hour hand on a wristwatch travels at 0.00000275mph.

- One thing that humans do more than anything in their entire life is sleep. Most Westerners sleep more than 6 to 8 hours a day, which is on average around 24 years of one's life!

- It takes about half a gallon of water to cook macaroni, and about a gallon to clean the pot.

USELESS STATISTICS

- A man's beard contains between 7,000 and 15,000 hairs.

- A hair is 70% easier to cut when soaked in warm water for two minutes.

- Women's hair is about half the diameter of men's hair.

- During an average lifetime, a man will spend 3,350 hours removing 8.4m of stubble.

- Four million children die each year from inhaling smoke from indoor cooking fires that burn wood and dung.

- Less than 1% of the 500 Chinese cities have clean air; respiratory disease is China's leading cause of death.

- The number of cars on the planet is increasing three times faster than the population growth.

- It took 1,175 animators working in Disney Studios in Burbank, California, Orlando, Florida and Paris, France to complete the animated *Tarzan*. Because of the time differences, production was able to occur around the clock for more than 3 years.

- The most expensive commercial ever made is one of the most famous. The 1984 Apple Macintosh commercial shown introducing Macintosh to the

USELESS STATISTICS

world ran only once during the 1984 Super Bowl. It was directed by Ridley Scott, and cost around $600,000 to $1 million to make.

- The average human eats 8 spiders in their lifetime at night.

- About 17% of humans are left-handed. The same is true of chimpanzees and gorillas.

- Banging your head against a wall uses 150 calories an hour.

- The entire length of all eyelashes shed by a human in their life is over 98ft (30m).

- No President of the United States was an only child.

- The average woman consumes 6lb of lipstick in her lifetime.

- It only takes 7lb of pressure to rip off your ear.

- $26 billion in ransom has been paid out in the USA in the past 20 years.

- You use more calories eating celery than there are in the celery itself.

USELESS STATISTICS

- On average, there are 178 sesame seeds on each McDonalds BigMac bun.

- There are 1 million ants for every person in the world.

- Odds of being killed by a dog – 1 in 700,000.

- Odds of dying while in the bathtub – 1 in 1 million.

- Odds of being killed by poisoning – 1 in 86,000.

- Odds of being killed by freezing – 1 in 3 million.

- Odds of being killed by lightning – 1 in 2 million.

- Odds of being killed in a car crash – 1 in 5,000.

- Odds of being killed in a tornado – 1 in 2 million.

- Odds of being killed by falling out of bed – 1 in 2 million.

- If you played all of the Beatles' singles and albums that came out between 1962 and 1970 back to back, it would only last for 10 hours and 33 minutes.

- Termites eat through wood 2 times faster when listening to rock music.

USELESS STATISTICS

- The Apollo 11 only had 20 seconds of fuel left when it landed.

- Thirteen people are killed each year by vending machines falling on them.

- There is a 1/4 pound of salt in every gallon of seawater.

- About one-third of American adults are at least 20% above their recommended weight.

- The average talker sprays about 300 microscopic saliva droplets per minute, about 2.5 droplets per word.

- The average smell weighs 760 nanograms.

- The Earth experiences 50,000 earthquakes each year.

- Even on the hottest days, skin temperature does not go much above 95°F.

- In 1994, 314 Americans had buttock-lift surgery.

- Experts at Intel say that microprocessor speed will double every 18 months for at least 10 years.

- The Earth's revolution time increases .0001 seconds annually.

USELESS STATISTICS

- Annual growth of internet traffic is 314,000%.

- Driving 55mph (88km) instead of 65mph (105km) increases your car mileage by about 15%.

- Airbags explode at 200mph (322km).

- A third of all cancers are sun-related.

- The average person flexes the joints in their fingers 24 million times during a lifetime.

- There are more than 1,000 chemicals in a cup of coffee.

- It would take 7 billion particles of fog to fill a teaspoon.

- Your brain weighs around 3lbs – all but 10oz is water.

- The average person makes about 1,140 telephone calls each year.

- The world record for rocking non-stop in a rocking chair is 440 hours.

- The world record for wellington-boot tossing is 179.14ft (54.60m).

USELESS STATISTICS

- Americans on average eat 18 acres of pizza every day.

- Fingernails grow nearly 4 times faster than toenails.

- You blink over 10,000,000 times a year.

- There are 1,525,000,000 miles (2,453,725,000km) of telephone wire strung across America.

- The average person laughs 15 times a day.

- The average person spends about 2 years on the phone in a lifetime.

- A can of SPAM is opened every 4 seconds.

17

USELESS
SUPERLATIVES

USELESS SUPERLATIVES

- The average Miss America Winner is 5ft 6.6in.

- The tallest Miss America contestant was 6ft 2in (Jeanne Robertson).

- The perfect height for a female fashion model is 5ft 9.5in.

- The perfect height for a male model is 6ft 0in.

- The tallest US President was Abraham Lincoln at 6ft 4in.

- The shortest US President was James Madison at 5ft 4in.

- The USS *Enterprise* was built in Newport VA and launched in 1960 and remains the largest warship ever built and the first nuclear-powered aircraft carrier. It is the eighth ship and the second aircraft carrier to be called *Enterprise*. At 1,123ft long and 250ft high, the ship is both the longest and tallest warship ever built. With a top speed over 30 knots, it is also the fastest carrier in the US fleet. Weighing in at 90,000 tons, the 'Big E', as it is dubbed by sailors, is home to over 5,000 officers and crewmembers.

- The only mammal where the female is normally taller than the male is a type of antelope called the Okapi.

USELESS SUPERLATIVES

- The largest web-footed bird is the albatross.

- On 31 July 1994 Simon Sang Sung of Singapore turned a single piece of dough into 8,192 noodles in 59.29 seconds!

- At 12 years old, an African named Ernest Loftus made his first entry in his diary and continued every day for 91 years.

- In 1925 Toronto, Ontario was home to the biggest swimming pool in the world. It held 2,000 swimmers, and was 300ft by 75ft. It is still in operation.

- The highest parachute jump ever made was on 16 August 1960 as a part of the Air Force research programme, Project Excelsior. Air Force Captain Joseph W Kittinger, Jr stepped off a platform raised to 102,800ft over Tularosa, New Mexico by a high-altitude balloon. To survive the altitude, Kittinger wore a pressure suit similar to those for astronauts. After 4 minutes, 36 seconds of free fall, he reached a speed of 714mph and became the only human to break the sound barrier without being enclosed in a machine of any kind. He dropped 84,700ft before opening his parachute, and landed safely 13 minutes, 45 seconds after jumping.

USELESS SUPERLATIVES

- In the original Ian Fleming books, the character Dr No was 6ft 6in tall. The character Auric Goldfinger was only 5ft.

- In 1876 the average Western man was 5ft 5in tall, 4in shorter than today's average. Half of that increase, a full 2in on average, has been since 1960 according to the US Department of Health and Human Services.

- Tsar Peter the Great stood 6ft 6¾in tall, an incredible height for the eighteenth century.

- The tallest bird alive today is the ostrich.

- With 252 lanes, the Tokyo World Lanes Bowling Centre is the largest bowling establishment in the world.

- The tallest mammal is the giraffe.

- The tallest snake is the king cobra, which can rear itself up to 6ft and spread its 'hood' 9in.

- The West Edmonton Mall, located in Edmonton, Alberta, Canada, is the world's largest shopping mall. The mall includes 5.3 million sq ft of space. There are over 800 stores, over 110 eating establishments, 26 movie theatres and 7 attractions, including an amusement park, waterpark, mini-golf, ice rink, the world's largest indoor lake and varied sea life. The mall

USELESS SUPERLATIVES

occupies 121 acres and the parking can accommodate 20,000 cars. The total cost for the 4 phases of construction for the mall topped $2.8 billion.

- The Giant Sequoia (*Sequoiadendron giganteum*) is the largest living organism on Earth, and is native, primarily, to the Sierra Nevada Mountains of eastern California. The largest Sequoia is the General Sherman tree with a height of 250ft and a diameter near the base of 24.75ft. The trunk of the tree weighs almost 1,400 tons.

- The tallest man on record was Robert Wadlow of Illinois, USA. He was 8ft 11.1in tall, and at the time of his death at the age of 22 he weighed 490lb.

- The tallest woman ever recorded, Trijntje Cornelisdochter, was born in 1616 in Holland. She was 8ft 4in tall when she died, aged 17, in 1633.

- The tallest married couple were Anna Hanen Swan (1846–88), and Martin Van Buren Bates (1845–1919). She was 7ft 5½in and Martin stood 7ft 2½in when they married at the Church of St Martin-in-the-Fields, London, on 17 June 1871.

- At 891ft tall, the 1.6 mile-long Millau Bridge is the tallest road bridge in the world. It crosses the Tarn Valley, in France's Massif Central mountains, opened in

USELESS SUPERLATIVES

2004. The suspension bridge hangs on 7 towers, the tallest being 1,122ft tall. It was constructed over 3 years at a cost of 394 million euros.

- Released in 2002, the sci/fi comedy *The Adventures of Pluto Nash* is the biggest Hollywood bomb in terms of loss. The movie had a gross budget of $100 million, but only earned $4.41 million at the US box office.

- The Caterpillar 797B dump truck is currently the largest in the world and has a load capacity of 380 tons. It is powered by a turbocharged diesel engine making 3,550 horsepower. It is 21.5ft tall, 28ft wide and 47.7ft long and has an empty operating weight of 278 tons. Each tyre is 13ft tall, weighs 4 tons and costs $25,000.00.

- The Cunard cruise ship, *Queen Mary 2*, launched in 2003, is the longest, tallest, widest and heaviest passenger ship ever constructed. The ship measures 1138.5ft long, 135.3ft wide and 237.6m tall, and weighs some 150,000 tons. The ship houses 2,630 passengers and features 5 swimming pools, 14 restaurants, 24 massage parlours and an art gallery.

- The CargoLifter hangar, located in Brand, Germany, on a former Soviet military airport, is the largest self-supporting hangar in the world. At 360m long, 210m wide and 107m high, the hangar was designed to

USELESS SUPERLATIVES

accommodate the planned CargoLifter CL 160, a 260m-long airship.

- The tallest manmade structure in the world is the CN Tower located in Toronto, Canada, at 1,815ft.

- The biggest hog ever recorded was a creature named Big Boy, who weighed in at 1,904lb.

- The Hindenburg (LZ 129), built by the Zeppelin Company of Germany in 1936, was the largest aircraft ever built and flown. It was 804ft long, with a maximum diameter of 135ft and boasted a 200ft-long promenade deck. The Hindenburg flew at a top speed of 82mph, cutting the trans-Atlantic travel time by more than two-thirds, and could lift 112 tons beyond its own weight. It was used in trans-Atlantic service for a year before crashing in May 1937.

- The average US adult male is 5ft 9.1in, but 3.9% of US men are 6ft 2in or taller.

- The average US adult female is 5ft 3.7in, but 0.7% of US women are 5ft 10in or taller.

- The minimum height for a US astronaut is 4ft 10.5in, and the minimum height for a US Space Shuttle pilot is 5ft 4in.

USELESS SUPERLATIVES

- The maximum height for all US Space Shuttle crew is 6ft 4in.

- The longest Monopoly game ever played was 1,680 hours long – that's 70 straight days!

- With faces standing 60ft tall and 500ft up, the Mount Rushmore National Monument is the largest art object in the world. The four faces of American Presidents George Washington, Thomas Jefferson, Theodore Roosevelt and Abraham Lincoln are carved into the face of Mount Rushmore in the Black Hills of South Dakota. Sculptor Gutzon Borglum began carving the mountain on 10 August 1927 and, along with 400 workers, worked on the monument until his death in 1941. It was never completed.

- More than a dozen writers worked on *The Adventures of Pluto Nash*, which features Eddie Murphy as a nightclub owner on the moon, struggling to keep control of his club when a wealthy casino owner tries to take over. It was shelved for almost 2 years before being released.

- The largest cabbage ever grown weighed 144lb.

- The largest book ever published was *Bhutan: A Visual Odyssey Across the Kingdom* by Michael Hawley in 2003. Each book is 5 x 7ft, 112 pages and 133lb.

USELESS SUPERLATIVES

The book, which costs $2000 to produce, is sold along with its easel-like stand for $10,000.

- The longest-running theatre play is the murder mystery *The Mousetrap*, originally called *Three Blind Mice*. It was written by Agatha Christie in 1947 as a 30-minute radio play to celebrate Queen Mary's 80th birthday. Performance number 20,807 on 25 November 2002 marked its 50th anniversary as the world's longest-running play. The performance was attended by the Queen, also celebrating her 50th year on the throne. The play has been seen by over 10 million people and performed in 44 different countries, and it is still running in London.

- The world's tallest mountains, the Himalayas, are also the fastest growing. Their growth – about half an inch a year – is caused by the pressure exerted by 2 of the Earth's continental plates.

- Belgian driver Jenatzy was the first to reach a speed of over 100km/h in his electrically powered car 'La Jamais Contente' in 1899.

- *Linn's Stamp News* is the world's largest weekly newspaper for stamp collectors.

- The Bible is the number-one book to be shoplifted in America.

USELESS SUPERLATIVES

- At the 2004 French Open, Fabrice Santoro and Arnaud Clement played the longest match since the open era of professional tennis began in 1968. The match began on Monday, 24 May but play was suspended in the fifth set when darkness fell. The game resumed the next day and Santoro finally beat Clement 16–14 to win the fifth set. The 71-game marathon lasted a total of 6 hours, 33 minutes on court.

- The heaviest man recorded was Brower Minnoch of Bainbridge USA, who was admitted to University Hospital, Seattle, saturated with fluid and suffering from heart and respiratory failure, weighing more than 1,400lb. After 16 months in hospital, he was discharged at 476lb, but was readmitted 2 years later after regaining almost 200lb. When he died in 1983, he weighed more than 798lb.

- The longest Monopoly game in a bathtub was 99 hours long.

- The smallest fish in the world is the Paedocypris progenetica, a member of the carp family, which is found Indonesia and Sumatra. It grows to 0.31in.

- The longest snake ever found is a reticulated python that was discovered in Sulawesi Island, Indonesia in 1912. It was 33ft long. The largest snake ever held in captivity was a python named Colossus, who lived at

USELESS SUPERLATIVES

the Pittsburgh Zoo in Pennsylvania and at the time of her death she was 28.5ft long, had a girth of 37.5in and weighed an estimated 320lb.

- The cheetah is the fastest mammal on Earth and can accelerate from 0 to 45mph in 2 seconds. Top speeds of 71mph can be maintained for up to 300 yards. The fastest cheetahs have been clocked at over 90mph.

- The world's largest weather vane sits on the shores of White Lake in Montague, Michigan. It's 48ft tall with a 26ft wind arrow and adorned with a 14ft replica of a nineteenth-century Great Lakes schooner.

- The world's largest coffee pot is located in Davidson, Saskatchewan. It measures 24ft tall, is made of sheet metal and can hold 150,000 8oz cups of coffee.

- The highest wind velocity ever recorded in the USA was 231mph, in New Hampshire, in 1934.

- The world's largest yo-yo is in the National Yo-Yo Museum in Chico, California. Named 'Big Yo', the 256lb yo-yo is an exact scale replica of a Tom Kuhn 'No Jive 3 in 1 Yo-Yo'. Fifty inches tall and 31.5in wide, the yo-yo was made in 1979.

- The largest school in the world is in the Philippines, with an enrolment of about 25,000.

USELESS SUPERLATIVES

- Victor Hugo's *Les Miserables* contains one of the longest sentences in the French language – 823 words without a full stop.

- The longest unicycle journey was from Chicago to Los Angeles. It was made by Steve McPeak in 1968 and took him 6 weeks.

- The biggest bell is the Tsar Kolokol which was cast in the Kremlin in 1733. It weighs 216 tons, but was cracked in an accident and never rung.

- Shakespeare's most talkative character is Hamlet. None of his other characters has as many lines in a single play, although Falstaff, who appears in several plays, has more lines in total.

- France had the first supermarket in the world. It was started by relatives of the people who began the Texas Big Bear supermarket chain.

- China's Great Wall, the world's longest wall, stretches for over 1,500 miles.

- During a game of tennis, Howard Kinsey and Mrs R Roark batted the ball back and forth 2,001 consecutive times.

18

USELESS FACTS ABOUT HISTORY

USELESS FACTS ABOUT HISTORY

- The Aztec Indians of Mexico believed turquoise would protect them from physical harm, and so warriors used these green and blue stones to decorate their battle shields.

- More than 5,000 years ago, the Chinese discovered how to make silk from silkworm cocoons. For about 3,000 years, they kept this discovery a secret.

- Because poor people could not afford real silk, they tried to make other cloth look silky. Women would beat on cotton with sticks to soften the fibres. Then they rubbed it against a big stone to make it shiny. The shiny cotton was called 'chintz'. Because chintz was a cheaper copy of silk, calling something 'chintzy' means it is cheap and not of good quality.

- The pharaohs of Ancient Egypt wore garments made with thin threads of beaten gold. Some fabrics had up to 500 gold threads per one inch of cloth.

- The Ancient Egyptians recommended mixing half an onion with beer foam as a way of warding off death.

- The Chinese, in olden days, used marijuana as a remedy for dysentery.

- Captain Sarret made the first parachute jump in France from an airplane in 1918.

USELESS FACTS ABOUT HISTORY

- *Scientific America* carried the first magazine automobile ad in 1898. The Winton Motor Car Company of Cleveland, Ohio invited readers to 'dispense with a horse'.

- The first paperback book was printed by Penguin Publishing in 1935.

- In 1956 the phrase 'In God We Trust' was adopted as the US national motto.

- Henry Ford flatly stated that history is 'bunk'.

- The first Eskimo Bible was printed in Copenhagen in 1744.

- The last words spoken from the Moon were from Eugene Cernan, Commander of the Apollo 17 Mission, on 11 December 1972. 'As we leave the Moon at Taurus-Littrow, we leave as we came, and, God willing, we shall return, with peace and hope for all mankind.'

- Values on the Monopoly gameboard are the same today as they were in 1935.

- John Hancock was the only one of the 50 signatories of the Declaration of Independence who actually signed it on 4 July 1776.

USELESS FACTS ABOUT HISTORY

- Virginia O'Hanlon Douglas was the 8-year-old girl who, in 1897, asked the staff of the *New York Sun* whether Santa Claus existed. In the now-famous editorial, Francis Church assured Virginia that yes, indeed, 'there is a Santa Claus'.

- The first dictionary of American English was published on 14 April 1828, by Noah Webster.

- No automobile made after 1924 should be designated as antique.

- The first US coast-to-coast airplane flight took place in 1911 and took 49 days.

- Escape maps, compasses and files were inserted into Monopoly game boards and smuggled into POW camps inside Germany during World War II; real money for escapees was slipped into the packs of Monopoly money.

- Incan soldiers invented the process of freeze-drying food. The process was primitive but effective – potatoes would be left outside to freeze overnight, then thawed and stamped on to remove excess water.

- False eyelashes were invented by the American film director DW Griffith while he was making his 1916 epic *Intolerance*. Griffith wanted actress Seena Owen to

USELESS FACTS ABOUT HISTORY

have lashes that brushed her cheeks, to make her eyes shine larger than life. A wigmaker wove human hair through fine gauze, which was then gummed to Owen's eyelids. *Intolerance* was critically acclaimed but flopped financially, leaving Griffith with huge debts that he might have been able to settle easily... had he only thought to patent the eyelashes.

- The Netherlands have many seas so people wanted a shoe that kept their feet dry while working outside. The shoes were called *klompen* and they were cut from one single piece of wood. Today the *klompen* – or clogs – are the favourite souvenir of people who visit the Netherlands.

- When airplanes were still a novel invention, seatbelts for pilots were installed only after the consequence of their absence was observed to be fatal – several pilots fell to their deaths while flying upside down.

- In 1893 Chicago hired its first policewoman, Marie Owens. While the city was progressive in its hiring practices, Chicago's female police officers were not allowed to wear uniforms until 1956.

- Limelight was how the stage was lit before electricity was invented. Basically, illumination was produced by heating blocks of lime until they glowed.

USELESS FACTS ABOUT HISTORY

- On 29 November 1941 the programme for the annual Army-Navy football game carried a picture of the battleship *Arizona*, captioned: 'It is significant that despite the claims of air enthusiasts no battleship has yet been sunk by bombs.' Today you can visit the site — now a shrine — where Japanese dive bombers sunk the *Arizona* at Pearl Harbor only 9 days later.

- Leonardo da Vinci could write with one hand and draw with the other at the same time.

- During the California Gold Rush of 1849 miners sent their laundry to Honolulu for washing and pressing. Due to the extremely high costs in California during these boom years, it was deemed more feasible to send the shirts to Hawaii for servicing.

- According to the Greek historian Herodotus, Egyptian men never became bald. The reason for this, Herodotus claimed, was that as children Egyptian males had their heads shaved and their scalps were continually exposed to the health-giving rays of the sun.

USELESS FACTS ABOUT HISTORY

have lashes that brushed her cheeks, to make her eyes shine larger than life. A wigmaker wove human hair through fine gauze, which was then gummed to Owen's eyelids. *Intolerance* was critically acclaimed but flopped financially, leaving Griffith with huge debts that he might have been able to settle easily… had he only thought to patent the eyelashes.

- The Netherlands have many seas so people wanted a shoe that kept their feet dry while working outside. The shoes were called *klompen* and they were cut from one single piece of wood. Today the *klompen* – or clogs – are the favourite souvenir of people who visit the Netherlands.

- When airplanes were still a novel invention, seatbelts for pilots were installed only after the consequence of their absence was observed to be fatal – several pilots fell to their deaths while flying upside down.

- In 1893 Chicago hired its first policewoman, Marie Owens. While the city was progressive in its hiring practices, Chicago's female police officers were not allowed to wear uniforms until 1956.

- Limelight was how the stage was lit before electricity was invented. Basically, illumination was produced by heating blocks of lime until they glowed.

USELESS FACTS ABOUT HISTORY

- On 29 November 1941 the programme for the annual Army-Navy football game carried a picture of the battleship *Arizona*, captioned: 'It is significant that despite the claims of air enthusiasts no battleship has yet been sunk by bombs.' Today you can visit the site – now a shrine – where Japanese dive bombers sunk the *Arizona* at Pearl Harbor only 9 days later.

- Leonardo da Vinci could write with one hand and draw with the other at the same time.

- During the California Gold Rush of 1849 miners sent their laundry to Honolulu for washing and pressing. Due to the extremely high costs in California during these boom years, it was deemed more feasible to send the shirts to Hawaii for servicing.

- According to the Greek historian Herodotus, Egyptian men never became bald. The reason for this, Herodotus claimed, was that as children Egyptian males had their heads shaved and their scalps were continually exposed to the health-giving rays of the sun.

19

Useless Facts about Inventions

USELESS FACTS ABOUT INVENTIONS

- Benjamin Franklin invented swim fins.

- The abacus was invented in Egypt in 2000 BC.

- The Greek mathematician Archimedes invented the screw.

- The parachute was invented 120 years before the airplane. It was intended to save people who had to jump from burning buildings.

- The first pull-top can was invented by Ermal Cleon Fraze in 1959, after he had to use his car bumper to open a can of drink.

- Kleenex tissues were originally invented to remove make-up. Maybe that's why they're still called 'facial tissues'.

- Roulette was invented by Blaise Pascal, a French mathematician and scientist.

- In 1916 Jones Wister of Philadelphia, Pennsylvania, invented a rifle for shooting around corners. It had a curved barrel and periscopic sights.

- At the turn of the nineteenth century, most light bulbs were hand-blown, and the cost of one was equivalent to half a day's pay for the average US worker.

—USELESS FACTS ABOUT INVENTIONS—

- The first brassière was invented in 1913 by teenage debutante Mary Phelps Jacob.

- The same man who led the attack on the Alamo, Mexican military general Antonio Lopez de Santa Anna, is also credited with the invention of chewing gum.

- The guillotine was originally called a *louisette*, after Antoine Louis, the French surgeon who invented it. It became known as the guillotine after Joseph Ignace Guillotin, the French physician, who advocated it as a more merciful means of execution than the noose or axe.

- Benjamin Franklin invented the rocking chair.

- Camel's-hair brushes are not made of camel's hair. They were invented by a man named Mr Camel.

- The modern zipper, the Talon Slide Fastener, was invented in 1913 but didn't catch on until after World War I. The first dresses incorporating the zipper appeared in the 1930s.

- Western Electric invented the loudspeaker, which was initially called a 'loud-speaking telephone'.

- The first VCR, made in 1956, was the size of a piano.

USELESS FACTS ABOUT INVENTIONS

- The Chinese invented eyeglasses. Marco Polo reported seeing many pairs worn by the Chinese as early as 1275, 500 years before lens grinding became an art in the West.

- The first commercial vacuum cleaner was so large it was mounted on a wagon. People threw parties in their homes so guests could watch the new device do its job.

- It has been determined that less than 1 patented invention in 100 makes any money for the inventor.

- The rickshaw was invented by the Reverend Jonathan Scobie, an American Baptist minister living in Yokohama, Japan, who built the first model in 1869 in order to transport his invalid wife. Today it remains a common mode of transportation in the Orient.

- The Ancient Romans invented the arch.

- The shoestring was invented in England in 1790. Prior to this time, all shoes were fastened with buckles.

- Maine was once known as the 'earmuff capital of the world', as earmuffs were invented there by Chester Greenwood in 1873.

USELESS FACTS ABOUT INVENTIONS

- The man who invented shorthand, John Gregg, was deaf.

- Because he felt such an important tool should be public property, English chemist John Walker never patented his invention – matches.

- In the year 1886, Herman Hollerith had the idea of using punched cards to keep and transport information, a technology used up to the late 1970s. This device was constructed to allow the 1890 census to be tabulated. In 1896 Hollerith founded the Tabulating Machine Company. Twenty-eight years later, in 1924 and after several take-overs, the company became known as International Business Machines (IBM).

- The first mobile car phones were located in the car's boot, taking up nearly half of the space.

- The Nobel Prize resulted from a late change in the will of Alfred Nobel, who did not want to be remembered after his death as a propagator of violence – he invented dynamite.

- Sylvan N Goldman of Humpty Dumpty Stores and Standard Food Markets developed the shopping trolley so that people could buy more in a single visit to the grocery store. He unveiled his creation in Oklahoma City on 4 June 1937.

USELESS FACTS ABOUT INVENTIONS

- The City and South London Railway opened the world's first deep-level electric railway on 18 December 1890, from King William Street in the City of London under the River Thames to Stockwell.

- The safety pin was patented in 1849 by Walter Hunt. He sold the patent rights for $400.

- The windmill originated in Iran in 644 AD and was used to grind grain.

- In 1832 the Scottish surgeon Neil Arnott devised waterbeds as a way of improving patients' comfort.

- American Jim Bristoe invented a 30ft-long, 2-ton pumpkin cannon that can fire pumpkins up to 5 miles at a time.

- Alexander Graham Bell applied for the patent on the telephone 3 days before he had got it to work. Had Bell waited until he had a working model, Elisha Gray, who filed a patent application the same day, would have been awarded the patent. But the telephone system we use is technically more like that described in Gray's patent.

20

USELESS FACTS ABOUT COFFEE

USELESS FACTS ABOUT COFFEE

- 'Coffee should be black as hell, as strong as death and as sweet as love.' – *Turkish proverb*

- The Arabs are generally believed to be the first to brew coffee.

- Fifty-two per cent of Americans drink coffee.

- An acre of coffee trees can produce up to 10,000lb of coffee cherries. That amounts to approximately 2,000lb of beans after hulling or milling.

- A scientific report from the University of California found that the steam rising from a cup of coffee contains the same amount of antioxidants as 3 oranges. The antioxidants are heterocyclic compounds, which prevent cancer and heart disease.

- Adding sugar to coffee is believed to have started in 1715, in the court of Louis XIV.

- Coffee trees produce highly aromatic, short-lived flowers producing a scent between jasmine and orange. These blossoms produce cranberry-sized coffee cherries. It takes 4 to 5 years to yield a commercial harvest.

- Australians consume 60% more coffee than tea, a six-fold increase since 1940.

USELESS FACTS ABOUT COFFEE

- Advertisements for coffee in London in 1657 claimed that the beverage was a cure for scurvy, gout and other ills.

- After the decaffeinating process, processing companies no longer throw the caffeine away; they sell it to pharmaceutical companies.

- After the coffee beans are roasted, and when they begin to cool, they release about 700 chemical substances that make up the vaporising aromas.

- An Arabica coffee tree can produce up to 12lb of coffee a year, depending on soil and climate.

- Hawaii features an annual Kona Festival, a coffee-picking contest. Each year the winner becomes a state celebrity.

- Beethoven was a coffee lover, and so particular about his coffee that he always counted 60 beans each cup when he prepared his brew.

- Before roasting, some green coffee beans are stored for years, and experts believe that certain beans improve with age, when stored properly.

- By 1850 the manual coffee grinder found its way to most upper-middle-class kitchens of the Western world.

USELESS FACTS ABOUT COFFEE

- Before the first French cafe in the late eighteenth century, coffee was sold by street vendors in Europe in the Arab fashion. The Arabs were the forerunners of the pavement espresso carts of today.

- Brazil accounts for almost one-third of the world's coffee production, producing over 3⅓ billion pounds of coffee each year.

- Caffeine is on the International Olympic Committee list of prohibited substances. Athletes who test positive for more than 12 micrograms of caffeine per millilitre of urine may be banned from the Olympic Games. This level may be reached after drinking about five cups of coffee.

- Citrus has been added to coffee for several hundred years.

- Coffee as a medicine reached its highest and lowest point in the seventeenth century in England. Wild medical contraptions to administer a mixture of coffee and an assortment of heated butter, honey and oil became treatments for the sick. Soon tea replaced coffee as the national beverage.

- Coffee is graded according to three criteria: bean quality (altitude and species), quality of preparation and size of bean.

USELESS FACTS ABOUT COFFEE

- Coffee trees are self-pollinating.

- Coffee beans are similar to grapes that produce wine in that they are affected by the temperature, soil conditions, altitude, rainfall, drainage and degree of ripeness when picked.

- Coffee is generally roasted between 400°F and 425°F.

- The longer it is roasted, the darker the roast. Roasting time is usually from 10 to 20 minutes.

- Coffee is grown commercially in over 45 countries throughout the world.

- Coffee is the most popular beverage worldwide with over 400 billion cups consumed each year.

- Coffee's popularity may be attributed to the fact that just about all flavours mix well with it.

- Coffee recipe from: *Kitchen Directory and American Housewife* (1844) 'Use a tablespoonful ground to a pint of boiling water [less than a quarter of what we would use today]. Boil in tin pot twenty to twenty-five minutes. If boiled longer it will not taste fresh and lively. Let stand four or five minutes to settle, pour off grounds into a coffee pot or urn.'

USELESS FACTS ABOUT COFFEE

- Coffee represents 75% of all the caffeine consumed in the United States.

- Coffee sacks are usually made of hemp and weigh approximately 132lb when they are full of green coffee beans. It takes over 600,000 beans to fill a coffee sack.

- Coffee trees are evergreen and grow to heights above 15ft but are normally pruned to around 8ft in order to facilitate harvesting.

- Coffee was first known in Europe as 'Arabian Wine'.

- Coffee, along with beer and peanut butter, is on a list of the 'ten most recognisable odours'.

- Coffee, as a world commodity, is second only to oil.

- During World War II, the US government used 260 million pounds of instant coffee.

- During the American Civil War, the Union soldiers were issued 8lb of ground roasted coffee as part of their personal ration of 100lb of food. And they had another choice: 10lb of green coffee beans.

- Frederick the Great had his coffee made with champagne and a bit of mustard.

USELESS FACTS ABOUT COFFEE

- Commercially flavoured coffee beans are flavoured after they are roasted and partially cooled to around 100 degrees. Then the flavour is applied, when the coffee beans' pores are open and therefore more receptive to flavour absorption.

- Dark roasted coffees actually have less caffeine than medium roasts. The longer a coffee is roasted, the more caffeine burns off during the process.

- Finely grinding coffee beans and boiling them in water is known as 'Turkish coffee'. It is still made this way today in Turkey and Greece.

- Flavoured coffees are created after the roasting process by applying flavoured oils specially created to use on coffee beans.

- 'Hard Bean' means the coffee was grown at an altitude above 5,000ft.

- Hawaii is the only state of the United States in which coffee is commercially grown, and the coffee is harvested between November and April.

- Iced coffee in a can has been popular in Japan since 1945.

- In Japan, coffee shops are called *Kissaten*.

USELESS FACTS ABOUT COFFEE

- If you like your espresso coffee sweet, you should use granulated sugar, which dissolves more quickly, rather than sugar cubes; white sugar rather than brown sugar; and real sugar rather than sweeteners, which alter the taste of the coffee.

- In 1670 Dorothy Jones of Boston was granted a licence to sell coffee, and so became the first American coffee trader.

- In 1727, using seedlings smuggled from Paris, coffee plants were first cultivated in Brazil. Brazil is now by far the world's largest producer of coffee.

- In 1900 coffee was often delivered door-to-door in the United States by horse-pulled wagons.

- In 1990 over 4 billion dollars worth of coffee was imported into the United States.

- In early America, coffee was usually taken between meals and after dinner.

- In Italy, espresso is considered so essential to daily life that the price is regulated by the government.

- In the sixteenth century, Turkish women could divorce their husbands if the man failed to keep his family's pot filled with coffee.

USELESS FACTS ABOUT COFFEE

- In Sumatra, workers on coffee plantations gather the world's most expensive coffee by following a gourmet marsupial who consumes only the choicest coffee beans. By picking through what he excretes, they obtain the world's most expensive coffee – 'Kopi Luwak', which sells for over $100 per pound.

- In the fourteenth century, the Arabs started to cultivate coffee plants. The first commercially grown and harvested coffee originated in the Arabian Peninsula near the port of Mocha.

- In the last three centuries, 90% of all people living in the Western world have switched from tea to coffee.

- In 1763, there were over 200 coffee shops in Venice.

- In 1790, there were two firsts in the United States: the first wholesale coffee roasting company, and the first newspaper advertisement featuring coffee.

- Irish cream and hazelnut are the most popular whole bean coffee flavourings.

- The first coffee mill appeared in London during the seventeenth century.

- Italy now has over 200,000 coffee bars, and still growing.

USELESS FACTS ABOUT COFFEE

- Over 5 million people in Brazil are employed by the coffee trade. Most of those are involved with the cultivation and harvesting of more than 3 billion coffee plants.

- Italians do not drink espresso during meals. It is considered to be a separate thing and is given its own time.

- Jamaica Blue Mountain is often regarded as the best coffee in the world.

- Japan ranks number three in the world for coffee consumption.

- Large doses of coffee can be lethal. Ten grams, or 100 cups over 4 hours, can kill the average human.

- *Latte* is the Italian word for milk. So, if you order a *latte* in Italy, you'll be served a glass of milk.

- Lloyd's of London began as Edward Lloyd's coffeehouse.

- Milk as an additive to coffee became popular in the 1680s, when a French physician recommended that cafe au lait be used for medicinal purposes.

- The official Coffee Day in Japan is 1 October.

USELESS FACTS ABOUT COFFEE

- Only about 20% of harvested coffee beans are considered to be a premium bean of the highest quality.

- Over 10,000 coffee cafes plus several thousand vending machines with both hot and cold coffee serve the needs of Tokyo alone.

- Over 53 countries grow coffee worldwide, but all of them lie along the equator between the Tropics of Cancer and Capricorn.

- Over-roasted coffee beans are very flammable during the roasting process.

- Raw coffee beans, soaked in water and spices, are chewed like sweets in many parts of Africa.

- Regular coffee drinkers have about one-third less asthma symptoms than non-coffee drinkers, according to a Harvard researcher who studied 20,000 people.

- Special studies conducted about the human body reveal it will usually absorb up to about 300mg of caffeine at a given time – about 4 normal cups. Additional amounts are just cast off, providing no further stimulation. The human body dissipates 20% of the caffeine in the system each hour.

USELESS FACTS ABOUT COFFEE

- Roasted coffee beans start to lose small amounts of flavour within two weeks. Ground coffee begins to lose its flavour in 1 hour. Brewed coffee and espresso loses flavour within minutes.

- Espresso vendors report an increase in decaffeinated sales in the month of January due to New Year's resolutions to decrease caffeine intake.

- Scandinavia has the world's highest per capita annual coffee consumption: 26.4lb.

- Italy has an annual consumption per capita of only 10lb.

- The 2,000 Arabica coffee cherries it takes to make a roasted pound of coffee are normally picked by hand as they ripen. Since each cherry contains two beans, it takes about 4,000 Arabica beans to make a pound of roasted coffee.

- The Arabica is the original coffee plant, which still grows wild in Ethiopia. The Arabica coffee tree is an evergreen and in the wild will grow to a height between 14 and 20ft.

- The average annual coffee consumption of an American adult is 26.7 gallons, or over 400 cups.

USELESS FACTS ABOUT COFFEE

- The aroma and flavour derived from coffee is a result of the little beads of the oily substance called coffee essence, coffeol, or coffee oil. This is not an actual oil since it dissolves in water.

- The first Parisian cafe opened in 1689 to serve coffee.

- The average age of an Italian barista is 48 years old. A barista is a respected job title in Italy.

- The average cup of coffee contains more than 1,000 different chemical components, none of which is tasted in isolation but only as part of the overall flavour.

- The drip pot was invented by a Frenchman around 1800.

- The coffee filter was invented in 1908 by Melitta Benz, a German homemaker, when she lined a tin cup with blotter paper to filter the coffee grinds.

- The coffee tree produces its first full crop when it is about 5 years old. Thereafter, it produces consistently for 15 or 20 years.

- The most widely accepted legend associated with the discovery of coffee is of the goatherder named Kaldi of Ethiopia. Around the year 800–850 AD, Kaldi was amazed as he noticed his goats behaving in a frisky

USELESS FACTS ABOUT COFFEE

manner after eating the leaves and berries of a coffee shrub. And, of course, he had to try them!

- The Europeans first added chocolate to their coffee in the seventeenth century.

- The first commercial espresso machine was manufactured in Italy in 1906.

- French philosopher Voltaire reportedly drank 50 cups of coffee a day.

- The largest coffee importer centre in the USA is located in the city of New Orleans.

- The heavy tea tax imposed on the colonies in 1773, which led to the Boston Tea Party, resulted in America switching from tea to coffee. Drinking coffee was an expression of freedom.

- The word 'cappuccino' has several derivations, the original of which began in the sixteenth century. The Capuchin order of friars, established after 1525, played an important role in bringing Catholicism back to Reformation Europe. Its Italian name came from the long pointed cowl, or *cappuccino*, 'hood', that was worn as part of the order's habit. The French version of *cappuccino* was *capuchin*, from which came the English Capuchin. In Italian, *cappuccino* went on to

USELESS FACTS ABOUT COFFEE

describe espresso coffee mixed or topped with steamed milk or cream, so-called because the colour of the coffee resembled the colour of the habit of a Capuchin friar. The first use of cappuccino in English is recorded in 1948 in a work about San Francisco. There is also the story that says that the term comes from the fact that the coffee is dark, like the monk's robe, and the cap is likened to the colour of the monk's head.

- The United States is the world's largest consumer of coffee, importing 16 to 20 million bags annually (2.5 million pounds), representing one-third of all coffee exported. More than half of the United States population consumes coffee. The typical coffee drinker has 3.4 cups of coffee per day. That translates into more than 450,000,000 cups of coffee daily.

- The vast majority of coffee, available to consumers are blends of different beans.

- Until the eighteenth century, coffee was almost always boiled.

- The word 'tip' dates back to the old London coffeehouses. Conspicuously placed brass boxes etched with the inscription 'To Insure Promptness' encouraged customers to pay for efficient service. The resulting acronym, TIP, has become a byword.

USELESS FACTS ABOUT COFFEE

- 'Those British are sophisticated people, in almost everything except their choice of coffee. They still drink instant ten-to-one over fresh brewed.' – Anon

- Turkey began to roast and grind the coffee bean in the thirteenth century and, by the sixteenth century, the country had become the chief distributor of coffee, with markets established in Egypt, Syria, Persia and Venice, Italy.

- Until the late nineteenth century, people roasted their coffee at home using popcorn poppers and stove-top frying pans.

- When a coffee seed is planted, it takes 5 years to yield consumable fruit.

- William Penn purchased a pound of coffee in New York in 1683 for $4.68.

- There are about 30mg of caffeine in the average chocolate bar, while a cup of coffee contains around 100 to 150mg.

21

Useless Facts about Food and Drink

–USELESS FACTS ABOUT FOOD AND DRINK–

- It takes a ton of water to make 1lb of refined sugar.

- The first product with a barcode to be scanned at a checkout was a pack of Wrigley's Juicy Fruit chewing gum.

- Lemons have more sugar than oranges.

- Some horticulturists suspect that the banana was the Earth's first fruit. Banana plants have been in cultivation since the time of recorded history. One of the first records of bananas dates back to Alexander the Great's conquest of India, where he discovered bananas in 327 BC.

- Carrots produce more distilled spirit than potatoes.

- Nutmeg is extremely poisonous if injected intravenously.

- Ninety-five per cent of the entire lemon crop produced in the USA is from California and Arizona.

- Banana plants are the largest plants on Earth without a woody stem. They are actually giant herbs of the same family as lilies, orchids and palms.

- A common drink for Tibetans is Butter Tea, which is made out of butter, salt and brick tea.

–USELESS FACTS ABOUT FOOD AND DRINK–

- A 1kg packet of sugar will have about 5 million grains of sugar.

- In a Washington study, 1 glass of water shut down midnight hunger pangs for almost 100% of the dieters studied.

- The Ancient Greeks called carrots *Karoto*.

- Lack of water is the main trigger of daytime fatigue.

- Americans consumed more than 20 billion hot dogs in 2000.

- Tobacconists in France used to put a carrot in their bins to keep their tobacco from drying out.

- An egg that is fresh will sink in water, but a stale one won't.

- As bananas ripen, the starch in the fruit turns to sugar. Therefore, the riper the banana the sweeter it will taste.

- Black pepper is the most popular spice in the world.

- Carrot flowers are also called Birds' Nest, Bees' Nest and the Devil's Plague.

–USELESS FACTS ABOUT FOOD AND DRINK–

- Britons eat over 22,000 tonnes of chips a week.

- Chewing on gum while cutting onions can help prevent a person from producing tears.

- Americans consumed over 3.1 billion pounds of chocolate in 2001, which is almost half of the total world's production.

- The carrot belongs to the family *Umbelliferae*. The cultivated variety is classified as *Daucus carota, variety sativa*.

- Both of the words in *Daucus carota* mean orange.

- Dandelion root can be roasted and ground as a coffee substitute.

- Germany produces more than 5,000 varieties of beer and has about 1,300 breweries.

- Lack of water is the main trigger of daytime fatigue.

- Goat meat contains up to 45% less saturated fat than chicken meat.

- Honey is used sometimes for antifreeze mixtures and in the centre of golf balls.

–USELESS FACTS ABOUT FOOD AND DRINK–

- Macadamia nuts are not sold in their shells because it takes 300lb per square inch of pressure to break the shell.

- Olives, which grow on trees, were first cultivated 5,000 years ago in Syria.

- A cluster of bananas is called a hand and consists of 10 to 20 bananas, which are known as fingers.

- The word 'banan' is Arabic for finger.

- A 1.5oz milk chocolate bar has only 220 calories.

- A 1.75oz serving of potato chips has 230 calories.

- A recent study indicates that, when men crave food, they tend to crave fat and salt. When women crave food, they tend to desire chocolate.

- American and Russian space flights have always included chocolate.

- American chocolate manufacturers use about 1.5 billion pounds of milk, which is only surpassed by the cheese and ice cream industries.

- A typical American eats 28 pigs in their lifetime.

–USELESS FACTS ABOUT FOOD AND DRINK–

- Bananas are one of the few fruits that ripen best off the plant. If left on the plant, the fruit splits open and the pulp has a 'cottony' texture and flavour. Even in tropical growing areas, bananas for domestic consumption are cut green and stored in moist, shady places to ripen slowly.

- The classic Bugs Bunny carrot is the Danvers type.

- It's a myth that Mel Blanc, the voice of Bugs Bunny, was allergic to carrots – he simply didn't like them.

- Aztec emperor Montezuma drank 50 golden goblets of hot chocolate every day. It was thick, dyed red and flavoured with chilli peppers.

- A honeybee must tap 2 million flowers to make 1lb of honey.

- In 1516 Friar Tomas sailed to the Caribbean from Europe bringing banana roots with him and planted bananas in the rich fertile soil of the tropics, thus beginning the banana's future in American life.

- Americans spend approximately $25 billion each year on beer.

- Holtville, California dubs itself the 'carrot capital of the world' and has an annual festival, now in its 55th year.

USELESS FACTS ABOUT FOOD AND DRINK

- An etiquette writer of the 1840s advised, 'Ladies may wipe their lips on the tablecloth, but not blow their noses on it.'

- Bananas are perennial crops that are grown and harvested year round. The banana plant does not grow from a seed but rather from a rhizome or bulb. Each fleshy bulb will sprout new shoots year after year.

- Aunt Jemima Pancake Flour, invented in 1889, was the first ready-mix food to be sold commercially.

- Americans spent an estimated $267 billion dining out in 1993.

- There are 100 to 150mg of caffeine in an 8oz cup of brewed coffee, 10mg in a 6oz cup of cocoa, 5 to 10mg in 1oz of bittersweet chocolate, and 5mg in 1oz of milk chocolate.

- California's Frank Epperson invented the Popsicle in 1905 when he was 11 years old.

- Capsaicin, which makes peppers 'hot' to the human mouth, is best neutralised by casein, the main protein found in milk.

- China's Beijing Duck Restaurant can seat 9,000 people at one time.

–USELESS FACTS ABOUT FOOD AND DRINK–

- Bananas have no fat, cholesterol or sodium.

- During the Alaskan Klondike gold rush (1897–98), potatoes were practically worth their weight in gold. They were so valued for their vitamin C content that miners traded gold for potatoes.

- The carrot is a member of the parsley family, including species such as celery, parsnip, fennel, dill and coriander.

- During World War II, bakers in the United States were ordered to stop selling sliced bread for the duration of the war on 18 January 1943. Only whole loaves were made available to the public. It was never explained how this action helped the war effort.

- Fortune cookies were invented in 1916 by George Jung, a Los Angeles noodle maker.

- In Eastern Africa, you can buy banana beer, brewed from bananas.

- Bananas were officially introduced to the American public at the 1876 Philadelphia Centennial Exhibition.

- Fried chicken is the most popular meal ordered in sit-down restaurants in the USA. The next in

−USELESS FACTS ABOUT FOOD AND DRINK−

popularity are roast beef, spaghetti, turkey, baked ham and fried shrimp.

- Goulash, a beef soup, originated in Hungary in the nineteenth century.

- To make haggis, the national dish of Scotland, take the heart, liver, lungs and small intestine of a calf or sheep, boil them in the stomach of the animal, season with salt, pepper and onions, add suet and oatmeal.

- Hostess Twinkies were invented in 1931 by James Dewar, manager of Continental Bakeries' Chicago factory. He envisioned the product as a way of using the company's thousands of shortcake pans, which were otherwise employed only during the strawberry season. Originally called 'Little Shortcake Fingers', they were renamed 'Twinkie Fingers', and finally 'Twinkies'.

- Carrot oil is used for flavouring and in perfumery. An extract of carrots was used to colour oleos (margarine) during the fats rationing that took place during World War II.

- In 1860, *Godey's Lady's Book* advised US women to cook tomatoes for at least 3 hours.

- In 1926, when a Los Angeles restaurant owner with

−USELESS FACTS ABOUT FOOD AND DRINK−

the all-American name of Bob Cobb was looking for a way to use up leftovers, he threw together some avocado, celery, tomato, chives, watercress, hard-boiled eggs, chicken, bacon and Roquefort cheese, and named it after himself: a Cobb salad.

- Rice needs more water to grow than any other crop.

- In Southeast Asia, the banana leaf is used to wrap food, providing a unique flavour and aroma to nasi lemak and the Indian banana leaf rice.

- Laws forbidding the sale of sodas on Sunday prompted William Garwood to invent the ice-cream sundae in Evanston in 1875.

- In 1976, the first eight Jelly Belly® flavours were launched: Orange, Green Apple, Root Beer, Very Cherry, Lemon, Cream Soda, Grape and Liquorice.

- In 1990, Bill Carson of Arrington, Tennessee, grew the largest watermelon at 262lb.

- Astronaut John Glenn ate the first meal in space when he enjoyed pureed apple sauce squeezed from a tube aboard Friendship 7 in 1962.

- The Greeks thought that carrots cured venereal disease while the Arab cultures thought it a possible aphrodisiac.

–USELESS FACTS ABOUT FOOD AND DRINK–

- In the United States, 1lb of potato chips costs 200 times more than 1lb of potatoes.

- Mayonnaise is said to be the invention of the French chef of the Duke de Richelieu in 1756. While the Duke was defeating the British at Port Mahon, his chef was creating a victory feast that included a sauce made of cream and eggs. When the chef realised that there was no cream in the kitchen, he improvised by substituting olive oil for the cream. A new culinary masterpiece was born, and the chef named it 'Mahonnaise' in honour of the Duke's victory.

- McDonalds and BurgerKing sugarcoat their fries so they will turn golden-brown.

- Mushrooms have no chlorophyll so they don't need sunshine to grow and thrive. Some of the earliest commercial mushroom farms were set up in caves in France during the reign of King Louis XIV (1638–1715).

- In Scotland, the Sunday before Michaelmas, 29 September, is called Carrot Sunday.

- India is by far the largest world producer of bananas, growing 16.5 million tonnes in 2002, followed by Brazil, which produced 6.5 million tonnes of bananas in 2002. To the Indians, the flower from the banana tree is

–USELESS FACTS ABOUT FOOD AND DRINK–

sacred. During religious and important ceremonies such as weddings, banana flowers are tied around the head, as they believe this will bring good luck.

- Nabisco's Oreo's are the world's best-selling brand of cookie at a rate of 6 billion each year. The first Oreo was sold in 1912.

- 'Colonial goose' is the name Australians give to stuffed mutton.

- Americans eat 18% more vegetables today than they did in 1970.

- Per capita, the Irish consume more chocolate than Americans, Swedes, Danes, French and Italians.

- Persians first began using coloured eggs to celebrate spring in 3,000 BC and thirteenth century Macedonians were the first Christians on record to use coloured eggs in Easter celebrations. Crusaders returning from the Middle East spread the custom of colouring eggs, and Europeans began to use them to celebrate Easter and other warm-weather holidays.

- On average, a baby in the United States will eat 15lb of cereal in their first year of life.

- The hottest chilli in the world is the Habanero.

USELESS FACTS ABOUT FOOD AND DRINK

- The Americans know the wild carrot as 'Queen Anne's Lace', 'Rattlesnake Weed' and 'American Carrot'.

- In an authentic Chinese meal, the last course is soup because it allows the roast duck entree to 'swim' towards digestion.

- Pine, spruce or other evergreen wood should never be used in barbecues. These woods, when burning or smoking, can add harmful tar and resins to the food. Only hardwoods should be used for smoking and grilling, such as oak, pecan, hickory, maple, cherry, alder, apple or mesquite, depending on the type of meat being cooked.

- Potato chips are American's favourite snack food. They are devoured at a rate of 1.2 billion pounds a year.

- Rice is the staple food of more than one-half of the world's population.

- In 1995 KFC sold 11 pieces of chicken for every man, woman and child in the US.

- Refried beans aren't really what they seem. Although their name seems like a reasonable translation of the Spanish *frijoles refritos*, the fact is that these beans aren't fried twice. In Spanish, *refritos* literally means 'well-fried', not 're-fried'.

–USELESS FACTS ABOUT FOOD AND DRINK–

- Americans consumed over 3.1 billion pounds of chocolate in 2001, which is almost half of the total world's production.

- A hard-boiled egg will spin. An uncooked or soft-boiled egg will not.

- Research shows that only 43% of homemade dinners served in the US include vegetables.

- Saffron, made from the dried stamens of cultivated crocus flowers, is the most expensive cooking spice.

- Sliced bread was introduced under the Wonder Bread label in 1930.

- Swiss steak, chop suey, Russian dressing and the hamburger all originated in the USA.

- Tequila is made from the root of the blue agave cactus.

- Jeff Chiplis, from Cleveland, has a collection of over 10,000 carrot items.

- The Agen plum, which became the basis of the US prune industry, was first planted in California in 1856.

- The longest carrot recorded in 1996 was 16ft 10½in.

–USELESS FACTS ABOUT FOOD AND DRINK–

- The Californian grape and wine industries were started by Count Agoston Haraszthy de Moksa, who planted Tokay, Zinfandel and Shiraz varieties from his native Hungary in Buena Vista in 1857.

- The colour of a chilli is no indication of its spiciness, but size usually is – the smaller the pepper, the hotter it is.

- The daughter of confectioner Leo Hirschfield is commemorated in the name of the sweet he invented. Although his daughter's real name was Clara, she went by the nickname 'Tootsie' and, in her honour, her doting father named his chewy chocolate logs 'Tootsie Rolls'.

- The heaviest carrot recorded in the world, in 1998, was a single root mass weighing 18.985lb.

- Potato chips were invented in Saratoga Springs in 1853 by chef George Crum. They were a mocking response to a patron who complained that his French fries were too thick.

- As much as 50 gallons of maple sap are used to make a single gallon of maple sugar.

- The difference between apple juice and apple cider is that the juice is pasteurised and the cider is not.

−USELESS FACTS ABOUT FOOD AND DRINK−

- The dye used to stamp the grade on meat is edible and is made from grape skins.

- The English word 'soup' comes from the Middle Ages word 'sop', which means a slice of bread over which roast drippings were poured. The first archaeological evidence of soup being consumed dates back to 6000 BC, with the main ingredient being hippopotamus bones!

- Pearls melt in vinegar.

- The US FDA allows an average of 30 or more insect fragments and one or more rodent hairs per 100g of peanut butter.

- The Greek foot soldiers who hid in the Trojan Horse were said to have consumed ample quantities of raw carrots to inactivate their bowels.

- The city of Denver in Colorado claims to have invented the cheeseburger.

- Americans eat an average of 18lb of fresh apples each year. The most popular variety in the United States is the Red Delicious.

- In early Celtic literature, the carrot is referred to as the 'Honey Underground'!

–USELESS FACTS ABOUT FOOD AND DRINK–

- Watermelon, considered one of America's favourite fruits, is really a vegetable (*Citrullus lanatus*). Cousin to the cucumber and kin to the gourd, watermelons can range in size from 7 to 100lb.

- The first ring doughnuts were produced in 1847 by a 15-year-old baker's apprentice, Hanson Gregory, who knocked the soggy centre out of a fried doughnut.

- The Japanese word for carrot is *ninjin*.

- The fungus called truffles can cost £450 to £850 per pound. They are sniffed out by female pigs, which detect a compound that is also in the saliva of male pigs. The same chemical is found in the sweat of human males.

- The hamburger was invented in 1900 by Louis Lassen. He ground beef, broiled it and served it between 2 pieces of toast.

- The herring is the most widely eaten fish in the world. Nutritionally, its fuel value is equal to that of a beefsteak.

- The best-selling chocolate bar in Russia is Snickers.

- It is alleged that Nero ate the last remaining root of the ancient carrot 'sylphion'.

USELESS FACTS ABOUT FOOD AND DRINK

- The ice cream soda was invented in 1874 by Robert Green. He was serving a mixture of syrup, sweet cream and carbonated water at a celebration in Philadelphia. He ran out of cream and substituted ice cream.

- The largest item on any menu in the world is probably the roast camel, sometimes served at Bedouin wedding feasts. The camel is stuffed with a sheep's carcass, which is stuffed with chickens, which are stuffed with fish, which are stuffed with eggs.

- People in Sweden eat about 1kg of ham per person each Christmas.

- The largest living organism ever found is a honey mushroom (*Armillaria ostoyae*). It covers 3.4 square miles of land in the Blue Mountains of eastern Oregon, and it's still growing.

- Popcorn was invented by the American Indians.

- Potatoes, pineapples and pumpkins originate from Peru.

- The vintage date on a bottle of wine indicates the year the grapes were picked, not the year of bottling.

- Milk delivered to the store today was in the cow two days ago.

USELESS FACTS ABOUT FOOD AND DRINK

- There is a carrot-pie flavour jelly bean!

- The white potato originated in the Andes Mountains and was probably brought to Britain by Sir Francis Drake in about 1586.

- The world's first chocolate sweet was produced in 1828 by Dutch chocolate-maker Conrad J van Houten. He pressed the fat from roasted cacao beans to produce cocoa butter, to which he added cocoa powder and sugar.

- Carrots have the highest vitamin A content of all vegetables.

- The world's deadliest mushroom is the *Amanita phalloides*, the death cap. The five different poisons contained by the mushroom cause diarrhoea and vomiting within 6 to 12 hours of ingestion. This is followed by damage to the liver, kidneys and central nervous system – and, in the majority of cases, coma and death.

- Van Camp's Pork and Beans were a staple food for Union soldiers in the American Civil War.

- Vanilla is the extract of fermented and dried pods of several species of orchids.

–USELESS FACTS ABOUT FOOD AND DRINK–

- Over 1,200 varieties of watermelon are grown in 96 countries worldwide. There are about 200 varieties of watermelon throughout the USA.

- There are more than 15,000 different kinds of rice.

- When Catherine de Medici married Henry II of France (1533) she brought forks with her, as well as several master Florentine cooks. Foods never before seen in France were soon being served using utensils instead of fingers or daggers. She is said to have introduced spinach, used in dishes 'à la Florentine', as well as aspics, sweetbreads, artichoke hearts, truffles, liver crépinettes, quenelles of poultry, macaroons, ice cream and zabagliones.

- When honey is swallowed, it enters the blood stream within a period of 20 minutes.

- Carrots are not always orange and can also be found in purple, white, red or yellow.

- When potatoes first appeared in Europe in the seventeenth century, it was thought that they were disgusting, and they were blamed for starting outbreaks of leprosy and syphilis.

- As late as 1720 in America, eating potatoes was believed to shorten a person's life.

–USELESS FACTS ABOUT FOOD AND DRINK–

- The white part of an egg is called the albumen.

- When Swiss cheese ferments, a bacterial action generates gas. As the gas is liberated, it bubbles through the cheese leaving holes. Cheese-makers call them 'eyes'.

- Carrots were first grown as a medicine, not a food.

- Although the combination of chilli peppers and oregano for seasoning has been traced to the ancient Aztecs, the present blend is said to be the invention of early Texans. Chilli powder today is typically a blend of dried chillies, garlic powder, red peppers, oregano, and cumin.

- Fresh herbs can be preserved by chopping them up and freezing them in ice-cube trays.

- A black cow is a chocolate soda with chocolate ice cream

- In South Africa, termites are often roasted and eaten by the handful, like pretzels or popcorn.

- Table salt is the only commodity that hasn't risen dramatically in price in the last 150 years.

- The milk of reindeer has more fat than cow milk.

–USELESS FACTS ABOUT FOOD AND DRINK–

- Grapes explode when you put them in the microwave.

- The Chinese used to open shrimp by flaying the shells with bamboo poles. Until a few years ago, in factories where dried shrimp were being prepared, 'shrimp dancers' were hired to tramp on the shells with special shoes.

- Native Americans never actually ate turkey; killing such a timid bird was thought to indicate laziness.

- Pigturducken is a pig, stuffed with a turkey, which is stuffed with a chicken, then deep fried in oil.

- Americans eat more than 22lb of tomatoes every year. More than half this amount is eaten in the form of ketchup and tomato sauce.

- The only food that does not spoil is honey.

- In Suffolk, carrots were formerly given as a remedy for preserving and restoring the wind of horses.

- A turkey should never be carved until it has been out of the oven for at least 30 minutes. This permits the inner cooking to subside and the internal meat juices to stop running. Once the meat sets, it's easier to carve clean, neat slices.

USELESS FACTS ABOUT FOOD AND DRINK

- Ancient Greeks and Romans believed asparagus had medicinal qualities that helped prevent bee stings and relieve toothaches.

- Worcestershire sauce is basically an anchovy ketchup.

- When tea was first introduced in the American colonies, many housewives, in their ignorance, served the tea leaves with sugar or syrup after throwing away the water in which they had been boiled.

- Worldwide consumption of pork exceeds that of any other type of meat.

- From 1lb of carrots, we can obtain 1oz and 11 grains of sugar.

- During the Middle Ages, almost all beef, pork, mutton and chicken were chopped finely. Forks were unknown at the time and the knife was a kitchen utensil rather than a piece of tableware.

- There are 2 million different combinations of sandwiches that can be created from a SUBWAY menu.

- The wheat that produces a 1lb loaf of bread requires 2 tons of water to grow.

–USELESS FACTS ABOUT FOOD AND DRINK–

- There are more than 7,000 varieties of apples grown in the world. The apples from one tree can fill 20 boxes every year. Each box weighs an average 42lb.

- Soy milk, the liquid left after beans have been crushed in hot water and strained, is a favourite beverage in the East. In Hong Kong, soy milk is as popular as Coca-Cola in the USA.

- There are professional tea tasters as well as wine tasters.

- There are thousands of varieties of shrimp, but most are so tiny that they are more likely to be eaten by whales than people. Of the several hundred around the world that people do eat, only a dozen or so appear with any regularity in Western fish markets.

- Thin-skinned lemons are the juiciest.

- Though most people think of salt as a seasoning, only 5lb out of every 100lb produced each year gets to the dinner table.

- Goat milk is used to produce Roquefort cheese.

- The Anglo-Saxons included carrots as an ingredient in a medicinal drink against the Devil and insanity.

- Sixty cows can produce a ton of milk a day.

–USELESS FACTS ABOUT FOOD AND DRINK–

- A mere 2% drop in body water can trigger fuzzy short-term memory, trouble with basic maths and difficulty focusing on the computer screen or on a printed page.

- It takes more than 500 peanuts to make one 12oz jar of peanut butter.

- In Australia, the number-one topping for pizza is eggs. The favourite topping in Chile is mussels and clams, while in the United States, it's pepperoni.

- Spinach is native to Iran and didn't spread to other parts of the world until the beginning of the Christian era.

- When American children were asked what they would like on their hot dogs if their mums weren't watching, 25% said they would prefer chocolate sauce.

- The dark meat on a roast turkey has more calories than the white meat.

- The most widely eaten fruit in America is the banana.

- The Chinese developed the custom of using chopsticks to eat because they didn't need anything resembling a knife and fork at the table. They cut up food into bite-sized pieces in the kitchen before

–USELESS FACTS ABOUT FOOD AND DRINK–

serving it. This stemmed from their belief that bringing meat to the table in any form resembling an animal was uncivilised and that it was also inhospitable to ask a guest to cut food while eating.

- Camel's milk doesn't curdle.

- Beetles taste like apples, wasps like pine nuts, and worms resemble fried bacon.

- The original recipe for margarine was milk, lard and sheep's stomach lining.

- Most common food plants contain natural poisons. Carrots, for example, contain carotatoxin, myristicin, isoflavones and nitrates.

- Chocolate chip cookies are the baked goods most likely to cause tooth decay. Pies, un-iced cake and doughnuts are less harmful to the teeth.

- Most nuts will remain fresh for a year, if kept in their shells.

- The Uruguayan Army won a sea battle using Edam cheeses as cannonballs.

- In 1987 a 1,400-year-old lump of still-edible cheese was unearthed in Ireland.

–USELESS FACTS ABOUT FOOD AND DRINK–

- Buttered bread was invented by the astronomer Copernicus. He was trying to find a cure for the plague.

- In 1983 a Japanese artist made a copy of the Mona Lisa completely out of toast.

- Washing a chicken egg will strip it of natural coatings that keep out bacteria; it will rot very quickly thereafter.

- During Thanksgiving and the Super Bowl, food consumption is larger than any other day in the US.

- A bee produces only one-twelfth of a teaspoon of honey during its entire lifetime.

- There are over 225 different kinds of bread in Germany.

- Humans are the only species who drink milk from the mothers of other species.

- Preliminary research indicates that 8–10 glasses of water a day could significantly ease back and joint pain for up to 80% of sufferers.

- China produces more apples than the rest of the world put together.

–USELESS FACTS ABOUT FOOD AND DRINK–

- Even mild dehydration will slow down one's metabolism by as much as 3%.

- It is illegal to import pork products into Yemen, with a maximum punishment of death.

- A single sausage measuring 5,917ft in length was cooked in Barcelona, Spain, on 22 September 1986.

- Over 180 million Cadbury's Creme Eggs are sold between January and Easter each year.

22

USELESS MISCELLANY

USELESS MISCELLANY

- Mount Everest was known as 'Peak 15' before being renamed after Sir George Everest, the British surveyor-general of India, in 1865.

- A 1991 Gallup survey indicated that 49% of Americans didn't know that white bread is made from wheat.

- At 7in long, the Wilson's storm petrel is the smallest bird to breed on the Antarctic continent.

- The first vending machines in the USA dispensed chewing gum and were installed in New York City train platforms in 1888.

- The fragrant patchouli is a member of the mint family.

- The white half moon under your fingernail is an air pocket. No one knows why it's there.

- More shoplifters are arrested on Wednesdays in January than any other time of the year.

- The stirrup in your ear, the tiniest bone in your body, is smaller than an ant.

- In its 120-day life span, each red blood cell makes 75,000 round trips to the lungs.

USELESS MISCELLANY

- The US military operates 234 golf courses.

- Vampire bats use rivers to navigate. They smell the animal blood in the water and follow it.

- There are 556 officially recognised Native American tribes.

- A cat has 32 muscles in each ear.

- The *Titanic* was running at 22 knots when she hit the iceberg.

- There are 2,598,960 possible hands in a 5-card poker game.

- Swans are the only birds with penises.

- When wearing a kimono, Japanese women wear socks called *Tabi*. The big toe of the sock is separated from the rest of the toes, like a thumb from a mitten.

- All owls lay white eggs.

- The names of the 2 stone lions in front of the New York Public Library are Patience and Fortitude. They were named by then mayor Fiorello LaGuardia.

- A broken clock is right at least twice a day.

USELESS MISCELLANY

- There are about 500 different kinds of cone snails around the world. All have a sharp modified tooth, which stabs prey with venom, like a harpoon. Most cone snails hunt worms and other snails, but some eat fish. These are the ones most dangerous to people. The nerve toxin that stops a fish is powerful enough to also kill a human.

- A pound of houseflies contains more protein than a pound of beef.

- Greater Auckland, New Zealand is the second-largest city in the world by area, the first being greater Los Angeles.

- Two-thirds of the world's eggplant is grown in New Jersey.

- In Texas, it's illegal to put graffiti on someone else's cow.

- Because radio waves travel at 186,000 miles per second and sound waves saunter at 700 miles per hour, a broadcast voice can be heard 13,000 miles away before it can be heard at the back of the room in which it originated.

- The country with the biggest percentage of female heads of household is Botswana.

USELESS MISCELLANY

- Orson Welles is buried in an olive orchard on a ranch owned by his friend matador Antonio Ordoñez in Seville, Spain.

- Kermit the Frog has 11 points on the collar around his neck.

- The Bronx in New York City is actually named after the Bronx River, which is named after the first settler in the Bronx – Jonas Bronk – who settled there in 1639.

- Before they became successful in show business, Charles Bronson and Jack Palance both laboured as coal miners, as did Ava Gardner's father.

- The Indian epic poem *The Mahabharata* is eight times longer than *The Iliad* and *The Odyssey* combined.

- A shofar is a ram's horn used in ancient times as a signalling trumpet, and is still blown in synagogues on Rosh Hashana and at the end of Yom Kippur.

- Chicago mayor Richard J Daley commemorated St Patrick's Day in 1965 by pouring 100lb of emerald green dye into the Chicago River.

- In response to the criticism that his reviews always praised Broadway openings, Walter Winchell replied, 'Who am I to stone the first cast?'

USELESS MISCELLANY

- While in Alcatraz, Al Capone was inmate #85.

- Bulletproof vests, fire escapes, windscreen wipers and laser printers were all invented by women.

- If Barbie were life-size, her measurements would be 39-23-33. She would stand 7ft 2in tall and have a neck twice the length of a normal human.

- The war of 1812 is the only war in American history of which Congress debated the merits.

- There are more Samoans in Los Angeles than on American Samoa.

- Soccer legend Pelé's real name is Edson Arantes do Nascimento.

- There are 2.5 million new gonorrhoea cases a year among Americans.

- If you could magnify an apple to the size of the Earth, the atoms in the original apple would each be about the size of an apple.

- Hong Kong has the world's largest double-decker tram fleet in the world.

- Hip-hop star Ice Cube's real name is O'Shea Jackson.

USELESS MISCELLANY

- There were 207 spottable mistakes in *Star Wars*, the most in any movie. Second highest was *Harry Potter and the Chamber of Secrets* with 203 mistakes, and third was *Pirates of the Caribbean: The Curse of the Black Pearl* with 201.

- On average, a hedgehog's heart beats 300 times a minute.

- More people are killed each year from bees than from snakes.

- Slugs have 4 noses.

- Owls are the only birds who can see the colour blue.

- The Mongol emperor Genghis Khan's original name was Temujin, and he started out life as a goatherd.

- Louis IV had a stomach the size of 2 regular stomachs.

- A scholar who studies the Marquis de Sade is called a Sadian, not a Sadist.

- Ralph Lauren's original name was Ralph Lifshitz.

- A person from the country of Nauru is called a Nauruan; this is the only palindromic nationality.

USELESS MISCELLANY

- Slugs use their slime trails to find one another. One cubic metre of garden soil can harbour up to 200 slugs.

23

USELESS FACTS ABOUT HOLLYWOOD

USELESS FACTS ABOUT HOLLYWOOD

- Marilyn Monroe's ex-husband Jo DiMaggio had fresh roses delivered to her crypt three times a week for 20 years after her death.

- The real names of Dean Martin and Jerry Lewis were Dino Paul Croccetti and Jerome Levitch.

- 'Her virtue was that she said what she thought, her vice that what she thought didn't amount to much.'
  Peter Ustinov on Hollywood gossip columnist Hedda Hopper

- A few witty remarks from comedienne actress Mae West:
  'Too much of a good thing can be wonderful.'
  'When I'm good I'm very good, but when I'm bad I'm better.'
  'There are no good girls gone wrong, just bad girls found out.'
  'When choosing between two evils, I always like to pick the one I've never tried before.'

- Inscription on Rodney Dangerfield's tombstone: 'There goes the neighbourhood.'

- The most copied noses in Hollywood are those of Heather Locklear, Nicole Kidman and Catherine Zeta Jones.

USELESS FACTS ABOUT HOLLYWOOD

- The longest film title was *Night of the Day of the Dawn of the Son of the Bride of the Return of the Revenge of the Terror of the Attack of the Evil, Mutant, Alien, Flesh Eating, Hellbound, Zombified Living Dead Part 2: In Shocking 2-D* in 1991.

- Pete the Pup, a pit-bull mix that appeared in the *Our Gang* shorts, had a fresh circle drawn around his right eye before every shoot.

- Only 3 dogs have a star in the Hollywood Walk of Fame: Strongheart, Rin Tin Tin and Lassie.

- Cary Grant had been offered the role of James Bond, 007, and refused it before the producers offered it to Sean Connery.

- It took four months to synchronise the 3-minute scene between live actors and animated skeletons in *Jason and the Argonauts*.

- The highest-paid animal actors are bears, which can earn $20,000 a day.

- The 1999 movie *South Park: Bigger, Longer and Uncut* has the dubious distinction of containing the most swear words in any film – 399 – and the most offensive gestures – 128.

—USELESS FACTS ABOUT HOLLYWOOD—

- The real names of Fred Astaire and Ginger Rogers were Frederic Austerlitz Jr and Virginia Katherine McMath.

- Film star Audrey Hepburn was fluent in English, French, Dutch, Flemish, Spanish and Italian, and was a member of the Dutch Resistance in World War II from age 15.

- 'Success is a great deodorant. It takes away all your past smells.'– *Elizabeth Taylor*

- *The Bridge on the River Kwai* won 7 Oscars, but they misspelled star Alec Guinness's name in the titles: they had Guiness.

- Leonard Nimoy owned a pet store in the 1960s before playing Mr Spock in *Star Trek*.

- 'The duration of a film should not exceed the capacity of the human bladder.'– *Alfred Hitchcock*

- In the movie *Rear Window*, Grace Kelly is in a scene arguing with James Stewart, who is sitting in a wheelchair with a cast on his leg. The cast switches from his left leg to his right during the scene.

- In the first *Terminator* Arnold Schwarzenegger had only 17 lines of dialogue.

—USELESS FACTS ABOUT HOLLYWOOD—

- The man who opened the world's first movie theatre in Paris said, 'The cinema is an invention without any commercial future.'

- In *Camelot* (1967) when King Arthur (Richard Harris) makes a speech praising his subjects and realm, he has a modern Band Aid plaster on his neck.

- Before he became a film actor, Humphrey Bogart, as the house player for an arcade, charged 50 cents a game to people who wanted to play chess.

- David Niven's voice had to be dubbed in on *Curse of the Pink Panther* by Canadian impersonator Rich Little. Niven was so ill while filming that he could not speak. It was his last role and he died the year the film was released, in 1983.

- Al Capone is shown living in a sumptuous Chicago mansion in the film *The St Valentine's Day Massacre*. In fact, he lived in a small house in a working-class district of the city.

24

USELESS LAST WORD

USELESS LAST WORD

TELESPHOBIA: The fear of being last.